CALLED TO TESTIFY

CALLED TO TESTIFY

The Big Story in My Small Life

JUDITH KALMAN

sh.
SUTHERLAND
HOUSE
TORONTO, 2022

Sutherland House
416 Moore Ave., Suite 205
Toronto, ON M4G 1C9

Sutherland House and logo are registered trademarks of The Sutherland House Inc.

First edition, May 2022

If you are interested in inviting one of our authors to a live event or media appearance, please contact sranasinghe@sutherlandhousebooks.com and visit our website at sutherlandhousebooks.com for more information about our authors and their schedules.

Manufactured in Canada
Cover designed by Lena Yang
Book composed by Karl Hunt

Library and Archives Canada Cataloguing in Publication
Title: Called to testify : the big story in my small life / Judith Kalman.
Names: Kalman, Judith, author.
Identifiers: Canadiana 20220169993 | ISBN 9781989555668 (softcover)
Subjects: LCSH: Kalman, Judith—Family. |
LCSH: Gröning, Oskar, 1921-2018—Trials, litigation, etc. |
LCSH: Children of Holocaust survivors—Biography. |
LCSH: Jews—Canada—Biography. | LCSH: War crime trials—Germany—Lüneburg. |
LCSH: Trials (Genocide)—Germany—Lüneburg. | LCGFT: Autobiographies.
Classification: LCC PS8571.A404 Z46 2022 | DDC C813/.54—dc23

ISBN 978-1989555668

For Évike
1938-1944

Unknown but not forgotten

CONTENTS

Coming to the Table

OPPORTUNITY SEIZED ME BY the throat in 2015. Would I testify at the Nazi war crimes trial of Oskar Gröning in Lüneburg, Germany? I cannot rightly convey the dislocation I felt, sucked from within the bounds of a world I knew and cast onto a plane of sheer implausibility. The notion that the extremely private tragedy that my parents had secreted away within the figurative compound of our family might somehow receive public attention exploded my sense of the possible. I shrank at the prospect. My parents had lost their large families in the Nazi Holocaust, and I had deliberately avoided Germany in my travels. Spending twelve days engulfed by the bludgeoning sounds I'd come to associate with the German language was but a small part of my dread. Yet urgency overtook me, never mind that a trial such as this had been seventy years in the making.

I first learned of Oskar Gröning on the day of Christmas Eve, 2014. A call from my sister Elaine, who was in Montreal, interrupted the preparations for the family gathering at my home in Toronto. She informed me that she had been invited to address his trial. Seventy years after the fact, a former SS official who had served in Auschwitz primarily as an accountant of sorts was being brought to trial for accessory to the murder of 300,000 Hungarian Jews between May 16 and July 11, 1944. During that time, he had occasionally served on ramp duty as the deportees were disgorged from the cattle cars. My sister was eligible to act as a co-plaintiff—a status akin to a witness—not through our mother, a former inmate of the camp, but through our half-sister, daughter of our father's pre-war marriage, a little girl who had been killed by Zyklon B gas along with her mother and our mutual cousins, grandparents, uncles, and aunts. The German legal system deemed her co-generational immediate family, although she had died before our births. Elaine was no more a survivor of Auschwitz than I was, yet she'd been invited to speak about the six-year-old victim my sister had dubbed our phantom sibling. This child arrived and perished in Auschwitz on June 3, 1944, among the 300,000 Gröning was accused of hastening to their deaths.

There was a lot to wrap my head around. My sister was not at first sure about getting involved. The defendant was so old. Internet photos showed a ninety-three-year-old man in a wheelchair, barely younger than our mother. In our minds, we pictured our aged loved ones: mother, aunt, our father's two cousins, all in their nineties. Although other photos of Gröning brought back a young, thin, bespectacled face under an SS hat, we somehow ignored the death's-head insignia above the visor and saw mainly the vulnerable face of a twenty-year-old boy.

Our late father's cousin, Zsuzsa, another survivor of Auschwitz, would take no part in it.

Not only did she refuse to testify in person, but she would not even agree to be interviewed. "At age ninety I can't afford to be turned inside out by going through all that again," she told us. "I've done my part." She alluded to the years of Holocaust education she had provided at her grandchildren's schools, and her interviews in the Spielberg Shoah project.

Zsuzsa was upset just considering the possibility. At our Christmas gathering, she trembled as her grandson suggested that he would accompany her at every step if she were willing to go. No, she would have none of it. She saw in Gröning an old man as frail as herself. Well-informed as ever, she pointed out that he had come forward in the journal *Der Spiegel* to denounce the Holocaust deniers. Gröning was not one of the worst, so why go after him? Why go after him now at his advanced age? Then she added, "And back then, he was just as gullible as the rest. Who of his generation would have dared not join the Hitler youth?" Indeed, was not the mercurial shaping during the late 1930s of the youth of Germany into an army of attack dogs in service of their master as much a genius of mass organization as the slaughter factories that would follow? She voiced thoughts I grappled with, and coming from an actual survivor, they were trenchant. Her daughter agreed, as did a friend in Budapest who had lost her Jewish father and later her leftist stepfather to the murderers and torturers of the Arrow Cross Party, the Hungarian fascist regime inspired by Hitler's National Socialists. They were leery of the motivations behind this new trial. Was it some kind of token scapegoating, too little and too late?

When I heard from my sister about her possible participation in the trial, I was certain of only one thing. If she went, I would have to be there to hear her honour our six-year-old sister's aborted life, to hear our sister Éva Edit's name spoken in a German court of law. "Don't wait for Elaine to go," said my Canadian-born husband of Anglo-Irish descent. His father had been among the Canadian naval forces that escorted Canadian troops during the Normandy invasion. "Find out if you might be able to testify for yourself. Elaine was asked because she's a writer, her background well-known. Probably no one in Germany planning this case even knows you exist." He went on to make the argument that ultimately made most sense to me: "It doesn't matter how old Gröning is now or how old he was then, nor what his personal reasons may have been. He wasn't conscripted into the Wehrmacht. Rather, he enlisted in the SS death squad voluntarily. He served in Auschwitz for two years. It wouldn't have taken more than two days to realize what was going on there. We can't absolve him of culpability because of his youth and the tenor of his times. Whether or not he regrets those choices now, or aided and abetted the greater crime from behind a desk instead of a rifle, he still facilitated a gross violation of human life by participating in any capacity in the slaughter of 300,000 innocents."

* * *

Between 2009 and 2016, two Nazi war crimes trials would follow the ground-breaking prosecution of John Demjanjuk, the Ohio former autoworker who was deported from the United States to Germany in 2009 to stand trial as an accessory to the murder of 28,000 Jews in the Sobibor concentration camp in occupied Poland. Demjanjuk died in 2012 before the court of appeals confirmed the guilty verdict found by the district court in 2011. Oskar Gröning and Reinhold Hanning, former SS officers at Auschwitz, would be tried on a similar charge. All three trials were due to the initiative of a retired judge, Thomas Walther.

On a morning in January 2015, my husband, John, and I prepared brunch for two German guests. By this point, my sister had put me in touch with Thomas Walther, who was representing many of the co-plaintiffs at the Gröning trial. He saw no reason why both of us shouldn't testify, and Elaine had come on board as well. Per Hinrichs, a journalist from the newspaper *Die Welt*, accompanied Thomas Walther to our home.

I had only once previously entertained a German national. Way back in the late seventies, when my father's cousin Zsuzsa's daughter brought to our flat in Montreal a German boy she had met on her summer abroad, my first husband, Craig, and I were as hospitable to him as to anyone else. Yet I recall one afternoon walk on Mount Royal during which this distant cousin and I spewed non-stop about the ordeals our families had gone through at the hands of the Nazis. The family narratives of expropriation, deportation, murder, and loss poured out of us, a tsunami of blame implicitly levelled at this sole, next-generation representative of his kind. The German boyfriend did the only acceptable thing he could under the barrage; he remained silent.

Thomas Walther was born in northeastern Germany in 1943. Acutely aware as an adult that had he been born to a Jewish mother in those times, he would likely not have seen his birthday, he identified, like many Germans of conscience, with those his country had persecuted during the thirties and forties. Before marriage, Thomas's father had hidden the families of two Jewish colleagues on his own premises. In his attempts to bring the few living former SS personnel to account while they were still physically and mentally fit to stand trial, Thomas Walther felt he was continuing in the footsteps of his father. He presented these facts as credentials while we broke bread. There was bread on the table, along with cheese and smoked salmon and cucumber slices, but my husband, accustomed through his work to hosting overseas guests, had also made his signature apple pancakes.

Throughout the meal, Thomas's voice predominated. In laboured English, he outlined the miscarriage of justice precipitated by the Frankfurt Auschwitz Trials of the 1960s, which had attempted to bring to justice all participants in Auschwitz who had implemented and facilitated, both directly and indirectly, The Final Solution. The law regarding aiding and abetting murder, however, had not been upheld. To arrive at a conviction, the court required the prosecution to prove the accused had had a direct hand in a particular murder. The mass killings could only be proved by each individual case, an impossibility.

One could only speculate as to why the law was deliberately misinterpreted, Thomas said, but it was likely political: to prevent a wholesale indictment of all who had carried out the orders of the National Socialists, and to protect former Nazis who had found positions of power after the war, within the government, the judiciary, and as leaders of industry. Oskar Gröning, among others, had been interviewed by the Frankfurt Prosecutor's Office on numerous occasions between 1978 and 1985 about his duties in Auschwitz. In 1985, these cases were abruptly closed for no apparent reason. It was hard to follow Thomas's detailed account because of the impediments of language on his part and contextual background on ours. What was most clear was that this was a man driven by the ticking clock: the advanced years of the defendant and co-plaintiffs, not to mention his own declining energies. Through my interjections, I sought common ground. We came from such different vantage points. He worked in the public sphere, whereas I was utterly private. What did

I know of Germans today that was not based on stereotype? And how could he know that he shouldn't make assumptions about me as a Jew?

I had the impression that Thomas Walther meant to take on the broken system he had served throughout his career. This may have been his primary aim, but I also began to feel that he wanted to give back in a restorative sense some tiny something of what the National Socialists in the name of the German people had stolen from six million Jews. Not only six million Jews. These six million that represent the Holocaust stood for the industrial methods applied to their genocide. But there were millions more murdered by the National Socialist regime and other genocides perpetrated by them against the Slavs, the Roma, the intellectually and physically disabled, the mentally ill, the Communists, homosexuals, and dissidents of the resistance.

Here at my table was the German baby born in 1943, blameless of the crimes of his elders. Just as I bore some of the trauma experienced by my parents, so had he, child of the perpetrating generation, internalized some of their guilt. Though unarticulated, we arrived at an understanding over breakfast. I opted to see that he was giving me the interview, not asking for it. He was giving me the opportunity to testify, the fact of the trial itself, and what he hoped would be the verdict. It was up to me whether to accept it and, if I did, what I would make of it. Thomas Walther with his video camera and Per Hinrichs with his notebook followed me up the stairs to the den where, I said, we'd get the most out of winter's pale light.

Spilling the Beans

THOMAS WALTHER AND PER HINRICHS had arrived on our doorstep in the worst snowstorm of the season. As John shook his hand, Thomas had quipped in heavily accented English about the Canadian weather. Commenting on the length of his trek from the Novotel in the northwestern sector of Toronto, his eyes wandered past John's tall shoulders as if seeking me out. He hadn't fully taken off his coat before levelling his first question. "Can you tell me? I am looking at the Google map to make my journey. And I am looking and looking for this street. Everyone else, all the co-plaintiffs, they are not too far away. Easy to go from one house to the other house, maybe just a little ride with taxi. But I must make the map go out to show the whole city. Then I see." Here his eyes engaged mine, and he raised one hand. "Everyone else lives over here," and dropping the other hand, "except this one, this Judit [he used the Hungarian pronunciation of my name] who lives exactly the other way. Can you tell me please why?"

He couldn't have guessed how nearly this question cut to the core of who I am, nor how long it would take for me to frame a proper answer. In fact, not until after the trial would I sit down at my desk to lay out my position.

* * *

John and I live in a recently built development within easy access to the city's pith. When we first started walking here, we were even newer to each other than the two or three freshly paved streets, their three-storey houses bald faced, yet-to-be landscaped, only intermittently lit by occupying lives. Over the months, our walks along these unclad streets would turn the ground of buried associations, much as our relation-ship would till our lives afresh. Memories of tender leaves on fledgling branches, fields of weeds and tadpole ponds, split-levels, bungalows, duplexes, fresh paint, and shiny soffits took root within me. There would be seven inhabited streets, the mud field of a promised park, and a pit bounded by hoardings for future development by the time we bought a house here. The demographic, certainly more diverse than the suburb of my childhood, reflects a culturally heterogeneous city: young fami-lies, retirees, White, Black, mixed race, Asian and South Asian, Middle Eastern, LGBT, Catholic, Protestant, Hindu, Muslim, and—true to the anomalous upbringing that shaped me—one Jew.

* * *

In October 1961, my parents bought their first house in Montreal in a freshly laid-out suburb of cul-de-sacs and scalloped crescents in the east-ern corner of the island city. The street was lined on one side by a long row of duplexes matching ours. Our half of the duplex consisted of a lower spacious flat with a basement, both accessed by an outer stairwell, as was the upper rental. Through the adjoining wall, the mirrored units housed an extended family of Italian immigrants who ranged between the floors, hanging out their laundry from the back balconies, and in the clement months, running up and down the spiral staircase bearing baskets of tomatoes and zucchinis harvested from the kitchen plot in the rear of their garden. In front of their house, a riot of dahlias filled the bed beside the plunge to the in-ground garage. On our side, my father had embedded chunks of grey Laurentian granite to host lichen, sedum, and spawning hens and chicks he called rock roses, either translated from

Hungarian or because that was the name he had learned in Britain where he had tended a tiered, tumbling rock garden to which ours in Ville d'Anjou was a pale allusion. I noted how the only immigrant families on our block, and all the streets I grew familiar with on my walks to school, ballet, and piano lessons, happened to live side by side. I never heard any language but French or English beyond our duplex and was frequently embarrassed by the volume of foreign voices issuing from the open windows at the Napolis next door, not to mention *chez nous* the Kalmans, despite my mother's hissed warnings to keep our voices down or the British tenants upstairs would think we were killing each other.

I was a latecomer to the grade-two class at Dalkeith School. It was my fourth school since leaving Hungary in November 1957. There had been an English nursery first, in the upscale London suburb of Purley, where we refugees of the 1956 Revolution had been offered a stately home essentially to house-sit free of charge by the headmistress of the school my mother's brother taught in. The nursery frightened me, separated as I was from my family for the first time, and also by language. A German shepherd presided over us with more rigour than the staff. It appeared that the British loved their dogs more than their children. I had watched in horror as the mother across the road threatened to pick up the telephone to call the child collector to fetch her little boy if he wouldn't behave. I pictured voluptuous, red-glossed lips on the mouthpiece beckoning something sinister out of the grey Purley mists. Next door, however, a listless, superannuated Georgie peed and pooed wherever he pleased, rewarded with a fresh bone from the butcher. The dog at the nursery didn't hurt anyone but the fact of its size, its stiff, bristly pelt, and sharp muzzle confirmed the darkness in its name.

In Canada, I attended a second nursery school and then grade one as a latchkey kid. I don't think anyone thought twice about switching my schools again. We were better off owning a home. We were better off in Canada where my mother could teach in the public school system instead of translating business letters in a Philips factory as she had in London. My father was better off here, too, as a bookkeeper rather than, at over fifty years of age, loading television chassis. England was better than Hungary where guns had been fired in the streets. Canada was better than England where immigrants with accents couldn't get jobs teaching in schools. Here we could say we were Jews without anyone losing a job. In England, a whisper about being Jewish might have led to my uncle's dismissal, notwithstanding the goodwill of his headmistress. If it was my fourth school in four years, what did it matter? The school was clean, well-appointed, the children decently dressed, and it had employed my mother to teach kindergarten. She was genuinely surprised to hear that I wouldn't stop snivelling.

The straw that had broken me was the intimidating word 'composition,' its grown-up sound full of unreasonable expectation. I had tried my best to adapt to changes, but this was the limit. Every time the teacher approached kindly with notebook and pencil and pictures of sunny barnyards or children playing hopscotch for inspiration, I burst into tears. Finally, she eureka-ed, "Why don't you just write something about yourself?" At which I rubbed my nose on the sleeve of my sister's outgrown cardigan, picked up the pencil, and, pressing its lead down hard so it wouldn't skedaddle, in approximate spelling I incised the words, "I was born in Hungry."

Given that early expression of my identity distilled from my nascent self under duress, why did I stop thinking of myself as first a Hungarian Jew identified by the land of my birth, and start saying I was a Jew born in Hungary? When did I give up both, joining ranks with millions of migrants who have ended up calling themselves Canadian? And how did I arrive at my notion of self as a product of history, happenstance, and genetics who claims no more than to be the grateful citizen of a hospitable state?

* * *

Sleeping dogs have laid low during the decades since I opened my eyes one rain-smeared Purley morning to peer into the meat-laced maw of the beast I dared not to call by name. Normally I sat immobile and silent on my pint-sized chair, afraid to make any inadvertent move the dog might mistake for invitation. I don't know how the chair tipped and upended me, but I did not assume that the avuncular tongue-hanging was out of concern for my well-being. A hot, stewy miasma stuffed both nose and mouth. Yellow fangs clicked above my eyes. I knew definitively what I had only sensed in the early days of my incarceration among strangers in this foreign encampment guarded by German shepherds. Didn't we hide our Shabbat candlesticks when the headmistress came to visit? Didn't we always say we came from Hungary without any mention of what had happened to my parents and their families in the war, as though the revolution during which no one close to us had been rounded up, enslaved, and gassed was the greatest crisis in our lives? Wasn't it obvious that the world was still not safe for Jews, that what had happened to my father's first little daughter, first wife, brothers, parents, and all those aunts, uncles, cousins, and their families—I wouldn't even start counting on my mother's side—was something shameful we the blameless had to hide, or else even the better world might bite us?

In 1957 and 1958, the years we spent in England, twelve years after the Nuremberg Trials, which had been headed by the British, the social climate in Britain still blew cold for Jews—immigrants and refugees of the war in particular. In March 2003, I flew to London to attend the funeral of my mother's brother, the schoolteacher whose headmistress had put a roof over our heads. He and his wife had had three sons, not raised as Jews, but neither as credibly Christian. The sons learned, in their teens, the history of their father's Hungarian family, most of whom ended up in the ovens at Auschwitz-Birkenau. My uncle had stayed in regular contact with his two sisters in Montreal, but there had been few visits across the Atlantic. My cousins' grown children regarded me with suspicion. What was this stranger doing at their grandfather's funeral? My aunt Jill wasn't sure about me either. I was there, I explained, to represent my uncle's two sisters—my mother and aunt—and our whole families. I'd brought photographs of everyone. My mother, aunt, and their British brother were the sole survivors of a family of seven children, their spouses, and their offspring. Now he, too, was gone. Was there really a need to explain?

The vicar gave the eulogy. Not a word was mentioned of my uncle's Jewish family murdered by the Nazis, nor of his two sisters in Canada who had survived Auschwitz, slave labour, Buchenwald, and a death march, before being liberated by the British. No wonder my English relatives looked on their Canadian cousin with distrust. Was I there to spill the beans? By contrast, to call ourselves Hungarian was acceptable. In grade school, I'd boast that I was born on the Pest side of the Danube. My friends looked at me blankly. The town of Pest, I'd repeat, in Budapest. Get it? Why I'm such a pest, ha-ha! The friends' last names were Spratt, Govern, James, Benoit, Marshall, and Fathers. What did they know about the map of Europe? When the word 'Jew' arose, a hot frisson ran up my back, scorching by the time it hit my face. This occurred rarely, but sometimes a classmate might say so-and-so had jewed him out of a dime or a nickel. It wasn't the insult that burned, but that private word uttered casually out loud. Being Jewish made me feel set apart. We were special by tragic history. We were the chosen people. We liked to believe we were smarter than most. And in our suburb, there were no others.

It's a little dizzying for me to note that I'm just one generation removed from the profound Orthodoxy of my father's family with its two kitchens, one for *milchig* and the other for *fleischig*. From his workplace on ethnically diverse St. Lawrence Boulevard, my father brought home to our white Wonderbread suburb fresh-baked rye, kimmel, and black pumpernickel, and deli meats made of pork innards veined with rivulets of fat: *kolbasz*, *hurka*, *Debreceni* sausages, salamis, and hams. Spiritually and emotionally, he belonged to the world of his parents, while his body, flung across first war-torn Hungary, then a continent, and later an ocean, had adapted like any organism bent on survival to what the new environments had on tap. Such a body-and-mind divide contorted one's self-image, I could only imagine, way beyond the distortions of a funhouse mirror. What was my little vertiginous head rush by comparison?

In the summer of 1964, my parents met with the rabbi of a Reform congregation in a posh, modern synagogue in one of the wealthiest areas of the city. It was way over on the west side of Montreal, requiring three buses and travel time of an hour and a quarter or more. As a family, we had taken this journey a handful of times in the previous year to attend a few holiday and Sabbath services. My mother was impressed by the chic modern décor, my sister by the cashmere sweater sets and camel hair coats of the college girls from Westmount, Snowden, Notre-Dame-de-Grace, St. Laurent, and Town of Mount Royal. My father felt less uncomfortable in the red velvet theatre seats, and with the integration of the sexes in the sanctuary, than by the fact that the men prayed bare headed. Not even on the *bimah* did the rabbi, cantor, or congregation functionaries cover their heads, not the merest *yarmulke* to be found among them. Here we were, finally among Jews, and my father in his broad, black fedora stood out as conspicuously as he did on the rattling Ville d'Anjou bus each morning. Recognizing the driver who picked him up at the same time on the corner of Boulevards Yves Prévost and Joseph Renaud, he would lift his hat by the crown and dip his long, Semitic nose in greeting, a decidedly old-world gesture.

I was sorry my father felt just as out of place in the newfangled sanctuary, but I rather liked getting to buckle up my patent leather party shoes to go to synagogue. Over the months, there had been discussion about the steep cost of tickets to the High Holy Days services, and membership dues. I had let these wash over my head. In retrospect, it felt that while I'd been performing underwater somersaults in a pleasant pool of trust that my family had reached a point of financial comfort allowing the luxury of a wealthy congregation, my parents had pulled a fast one on me. Gullibly, I fell for their invitation to accompany them to the synagogue for their meeting with the rabbi to discuss the terms of our membership. I browsed through the synagogue shop admiring the mosaic and enamel inlays on the brass menorahs from Israel, and the silver chalices and mother-of-pearl-handled knives for the Shabbat wine and challah. When my mother called me into the rabbi's office, she looked pleased, and I didn't know whether to be proud or embarrassed that she'd cut an advantageous deal with the cleric. He got up to introduce himself and shook my hand. "We look forward to having you in Mr. Shore's grade five class this September. Welcome to Temple Emmanuel Religious School."

It wasn't as bad as having to leave behind my current schoolmates. The three-and-a-half-hour weekly commitment was to expose me to—in order to develop a taste for—the company of 'my own kind.' The assimilated North American Jewish children I met at religious school downtown proved, however, to be nothing like us. They had TVs in their bedrooms and three-car garages, and rode roughshod over our religious school teachers with a dismissive disregard, which today we call disrespecting, but my mother would have pegged as bigmouthed. When Mr. Shore brought in pictures from articles that showed Jews in striped pyjamas behind barbed wire and far worse, I froze, much as I did at school when I heard the word 'Jew' bandied as an epithet. My Jewish classmates poured over the photos avidly, adding choice gruesome tidbits they had heard about, and for once not acting bored or mouthy but enthusiastically interested. Eagerly interested, as one can only be about something that has nothing to do with you and is compellingly entertaining in its horror. Nothing since has made me feel less among my kind, and more Jewish. It dawned on me that I was a Jew as one can be only when born from the ashes of the sacrificed dead, branded by the iron of history.

Around this time, I transposed my ethnic descriptor, placing the Jewish part foremost. There were two things I actually loved about going to religious school—the bus rides there and back. The pleasure going was qualified by the dread of arrival, but the rides back were enhanced by the snack of a York dark chocolate bar meant to tide me over for the feast of Hungarian blood sausage, *hurka* (how's that for cultural dissonance?), which awaited me in reward for enduring yet another session of religious school. Together they offered hours of observation of the city revealed along Sherbrooke Street, which crossed a large breadth of the island from east to west. I loved nothing better than the switch at Pie IX (pronounced always in French) from the eastern 185 route to the number 24 that bore me through the historic neighbourhoods towards the cosmopolitan centre. My parents may have felt vindicated in their decision to send me forth to discover children of another class and community when I insisted we give up our Christmas tree and exchange gifts at Chanukah instead. Until then, Christmas with my aunt's Presbyterian family had been the focal point of a season otherwise merely marked by chocolate Chanukah gelt. I admired the city west of Pie IX. It seemed to hold more substance and gravitas than our new bungalows and the Dairy Queens and Dunkin' Donuts along Sherbrooke East. But eventually, I would ride past the Temple, all the way to the university at the end of the 24's route, and as though that thrust westward had entered my bloodstream, I didn't stop until life took me across the different provinces. By then I'd finished graduate school and married a gentile boy from the West Island, as I think I'd been destined to from the start. After all, I did not grow up among Jews. My best friends, including my beloved cousin Pauline, were not Jewish. Even as I had walked down the centre aisle of the sanctuary during my Confirmation ceremony in grade nine, wearing a white robe and carrying a bouquet of red roses, I had done so cynically, already a confirmed non-believer, with my eyelinered, Twiggy-lashed eye to the main chance of delivery forevermore from the alienating world of my kind.

* * *

Contradictions of identity were a hallmark of my upbringing. We came to Canada from England so my parents could have white-collar jobs and openly practise their religion. Yet we lived among gentiles. Our Christmas tree, until I nixed it, sat in the front picture window of the living room, the curtains left open so its lights might be enjoyed from the street. But my father closed the dining-room curtains before we lit the Shabbat candles. My parents feared not for our own exposure but that of the family we were closest to. My uncle's and aunt's response to Holocaust trauma was to erase the past. Whereas my parents spoke to us of the past incessantly, my uncle and aunt hid it. They had converted to Christianity when they left post-war Hungary for Paris and then Montreal. They were active in a French-Canadian Presbyterian congregation, raising their family in that faith and also ignorant about who their parents had come from or what they had endured. We lived in the east end, so my aunt's family could visit us freely without fear of 'endangerment.' During childhood, my cousin Pauline was my best friend. Before she came over, my mother would remind me to put my religious school books in a place where Pauline wouldn't come across them. There was a spot I used in the deep closet of my bedroom, behind my mother's stored eiderdowns and clothes that weren't in season. On the one hand, I was being asked to cultivate a taste for the company of my own people and, on the other, to hide who we were from my closest kith and kin.

What did I think as a child about being asked to protect my cousin from my identity? It was like handing her a Kevlar vest while sending me into action without one. I didn't fault her or feel any real threat. My parents said that my aunt and uncle were unreasonably paranoid given the open society we enjoyed in Canada, so I felt sorry that Pauline's life lacked the depth of mine, as in knowing where we came from and how our parents had come to be who they were.

My cousins cultivated a lack of interest in the past that may have been in response to the tacit warnings flashed by their parents: DON'T GO THERE! pulsating in neon. They didn't ask about grandparents, for instance, or wonder why we didn't join them for church every Sunday. I resented the inconvenience of having to tidy away incriminating evidence before Pauline came over, and it made me angry at my uncle who was chiefly behind the subterfuge. He had resented the impoverished, repressive parochialism of his childhood home. Denying and forgetting it was a second liberation that perhaps did not cost him much. I speculate here. But my mother and aunt came from a happy family and idyllic childhood landscape through which they loved to roam when my uncle and cousins were not in earshot. My sister and I were privy to these amusing anecdotes about the antics of seven children allowed free range of the Jewish neighbourhood in their Hungarian town on the eastern border with Ukraine. But we were also upended by sudden reversals that landed us in Auschwitz or on a death march or under a bombardment of Allied fighter planes. My aunt felt no compunction about pouring her nightmarish reminiscences into the tender ears of her nieces. My cousins were to be sheltered, while my sister and I were slapped around by the flashbacks the two survivors wallowed in like a guilty pleasure. It made me much angrier at my uncle, although he never spoke of his own trials, because it was he who had forced my aunt to excise what was also beautiful from her past. I don't think my uncle trusted me with their secret, although as a child I was obedient and never once 'inadvertently' left a Hebrew copybook lying around. My cousin Pauline was quiet by nature, whereas my aunt dubbed me *kocs-kocs* which is Hungarian for chatterbox. Perhaps he mistrusted my spilling over with stories and opinions.

In the 1970s, I took to making my own clothes because much of what I wanted to wear couldn't be found in my uncle's ladies' boutiques or in our shopping centre. I liked the long peasant skirts, loose batik blouses, and African-print dashikis smelling of incense and patchouli sold in stores downtown among the smoked meat delis. My mother certainly wouldn't have spent a penny on these outlandish get-ups when respectable outfits were available to us at reduced cost, or free, from my aunt. When I could get my hands on fabric lying around, I'd fashion something loose, flowing, and long from it. Out of a trunk in the basement, I unearthed a pair of burgundy brocade antimacassars my mother had used to cover the threadbare armchairs passed down from my aunt for our first Canadian apartment. In my innocence, I made identical flowing tops, an ironic tip of the hat to a childhood of matching outfits: the shiny, green snowsuits with hoods that zipped open at the crown; the bathing suits, Pauline's blue trimmed in white and mine a red version; skirted sailor ensembles we wore at the same time, Pauline the little blond cousin and me the brunette. I was sixteen when I made us the 'hippie' tops. We weren't close after that. The virulence against me by my open-hearted, generous aunt was unleashed out of left field. She called me every salacious Hungarian invective and forbade me from hanging out with her daughter again.

You may well ask where that came from. It's difficult to control children once they become teenagers, especially when the slogans of the time exhort them to rebellion. Nothing seemed to flaunt my defiance as much as my refusal to model the tasteful wardrobe available in my uncle's shops and to sport rags instead. That I had extended such a rag to Pauline made my aunt and uncle see red at every pass. If they were afraid that I would try to turn Pauline into a Jew as I had tried to dress her as a hippie, they couldn't have been more offtrack. But the issue of Jewishness was a track Pauline's parents were as stuck on as the cattle cars that had relentlessly drawn them and their families to Auschwitz. That I had given up my practice as a Jew the moment I returned my Confirmation gown to the cubby at the Temple was of no reassurance. That, too, was a sign of my unreliable nature.

I have often pondered the pros and cons of the way my sister and I were brought up with a singular connection to the tragic past and how my cousins were raised ignorantly free of its grip. There's no perfect way to prepare children for a world rife with conflict and contradiction.

Once I had lost Pauline's friendship, there was no fear left of jeopardizing it. I also felt no further obligation to hide my family's identity. It had seemed to me an unreasonable expectation from the moment I'd heard as a five-year-old new arrival that my uncle had demanded my parents to forsake their religion as he and my aunt had done. This my parents couldn't stomach, although they did promise not to draw undue notice to our Jewishness, which informed where we would live and how circumspect we would be about our traditions. Their promise, not mine, I decided, unzipping our story from the secret compartment in the fringed pouch of my heart. I shared it with my closest friends. It was, after all, the story that governed my life.

La Campagne

L AC MASKINONGÉ IS A pool hardly more than two kilometres wide at the foot of Mont Tremblant in the heart of the Laurentians. This is where, as a small immigrant child in 1960, I had my first taste of the Canadian wilderness. We went raspberry picking, my mother and aunt, their four children in tow carrying sand buckets and kitchen colanders. The bushes along the dirt road around the lake were so dense with fat, dusty berries, we filled the pails and our tummies to boot, still leaving plenty for bears. What my mother and aunt, artists of Hungarian-Viennese cuisine, produced of those berries in the primitive kitchens of our cabins was never to be replicated: an elixir of fruit and frothy cream, a quintessence of raspberry whisked by a lowly fork in my mother's hand and a manual egg beater in my aunt's, the quarts and quarts of which we were ordered to consume before they spoiled, the slope-shouldered cottage fridges being too small to contain them. Not a drop were we to waste given the elbow grease expended.

At this time, both families rented their cottages, and I believe we might have returned to them one more summer before my aunt and uncle built their first holiday home. My aunt's cottage was on the north side of the lake; ours, smaller and less expensive, like everything we were to accrue over the years, more or less faced them from the opposite shore. Their cottage came with a rowboat, and my cousins would paddle straight across to see us. My mother and aunt liked to walk briskly around the lake for exercise. My uncle never walked anywhere.

During the week, he was in the city managing their three east-end ladieswear shops. My father, with us for the full single week of holiday to which he was entitled, strolled in the evenings after dinner, probably not all the way to my aunt's, but back and forth over a moderate length of the dusty track. He spent the days reading the Hungarian novels of Hans Habe and Magda Szabo or, more laboriously in English, Chaim Potok and Bernard Malamud, kept company by my sister, six years my senior, who, after acquiring her second language, would not pry her nose out of a book, as our mother's scorn-laden voice decried. My father helped my mother in the kitchen peeling potatoes and carrots and setting the table as an indulgence to his daughters, also to his wife's disapproval. On a particularly hot afternoon, he might go so far as to immerse himself in the lake, never deeper than his rounded middle, simply to cool off before retiring once more to the deck chair on the sparse, weed-spiked lawn. I cannot recall my father in bathing trunks. He must have taken his dip in Bermuda shorts, after first peeling off the knee socks he wore in all seasons.

Being in the country gave me almost unlimited access to my cousin Pauline, whose availability in the city was carefully rationed by my uncle. We were the same age but went to different schools. Her brother, two years older, loved nothing more than to disrupt our play by turning over the Snakes and Ladders board or barging in while we played dress-up, mocking each word we said by repeating it at top volume and pre-empting further amusement. I wish I could say he was lonely and jealous, but he was forever thus, with or without friends (which he never lacked) at his side. He was a spoiler by temperament, selfish and willful.

Pauline didn't judge his behaviour any more than she did her father's whose rules were arbitrary and whose vague objections to our getting together required bribery in the form of a hundred kisses each to buy off. The transaction rankled me, especially since my uncle seemed no more to enjoy my remittance than I did in paying up. I submitted for Pauline's sake. She was a golden child, as sweet as her brother was spiteful.

My cousins had been invited for lunch. My mother had promised potato pancakes. In our home we called these *latkes*, but at my aunt's they were the Hungarian for potato pancakes. Not that my cousins understood the difference because they didn't speak either Hungarian or Yiddish but rather English and French. Potato pancakes being on offer, the afternoon was to have been spent on our side of the dividing waters. I can't imagine my uncle would have offered to drive them, regardless of the weather, because he stood on principle about protecting his children from our religious contagion. Although he may have chosen not to stand in the way of the luncheon appointment, he would not have gone so far as to help it along. My father could forgive my lovable aunt all. In any case, he would have said a woman might be excused because women are weak, despite daily reminders to the contrary of my mother's steely drive and lacerating tongue. Nonetheless, he would have leapt to absolve my aunt of poor judgment because of her womanly giving-ness, in this case giving-in-ness. A man had to have known better.

My older cousin, having set his mind on potato pancakes, would not be dissuaded. He dragged Pauline with him in his favourite form of transport. We watched them, four of us glued to the window. Their image, water-warped by the downpour, rocked in and out. We focused hard, as if only our concerted gaze would keep them afloat. The size of the waves seemed out of all proportion to the small lake, its waters black and foaming. Two tiny figures pulled hard, two arms to each oar, Pauline's rain-hatted head a step lower than her brother's. She would have been seven years old maybe, and her brother nine. As we watched, my father cursed. My mother had a tendency to screech foul language and hit high anxiety on a dime, but my father was slow to burn. That she now railed against her sister's bird-brained compliance to everyone's will but her own was of no surprise. My father's anger, so different from his typical grandfatherly forbearance, was the more disturbing. He muttered in Hungarian, fists clenched. Those hands, always available when a dog loped towards me on the street, had retracted along with any attention to me, the cherished child. Surely, my cousins couldn't be in actual danger if my aunt and uncle had let them go. Already I knew to second-guess my parents regarding risk. They never opened the front door without peeking out through the safety chain even if the oil truck or bakery van had just pulled up. At my Canadian friends' homes, only the screen doors swung shut. We'd call out our names and waltz right in. If a friend's dad gave me a lift to swim lessons, my father held me back from running out to the car. He'd step forward first to introduce himself formally and to appraise the driver, making it plain that I was a monitored child.

He stood transfixed at the streaming window glass. When the row-boat pulled ashore, he pounced into the welter, grabbed each cousin by the arm, yanking them under our roof. They shook themselves like dogs in the small kitchen, laughing off the adventure. I think now perhaps this was the reason we didn't holiday again with my aunt's family. I would spend many summers on my own at the country house they'd build in St. Sauveur and my mother and sister would occasionally go up for a few days at a time. My father found some excuse not to go until much later, after he retired and, perhaps not coincidentally, only once my uncle had died. I don't think my father ever forgave his brother-in-law for play-ing fast and loose with his children's lives. My uncle, whatever deprivations he had suffered, had not, like his brother-in-law, lost a child to Auschwitz.

The only other country place my parents rented was after we gave up joining my aunt's family in St. Jovite. We came to it through Mrs. Reed, my school's librarian. She and my mother, the kindergarten teacher, were lunchroom friends. The Reeds lived beside the Benoits, who owned the cottage on the Ouareau River in Rawdon, and because we didn't own a car, Mr. Benoit offered to drive us up to Rawdon for our holiday week. On the way up, he said he knew an elderly lady who lived near Rawdon. We might be interested in stopping by to meet her.

We were a verbal, not an artistic family. My father was an engaging raconteur, I a loudmouth, my mother a shrieker, my sister a born pundit. We had a tendency to all speak at once, each of us raising the volume to be heard above the rest until one solitary peal was left declaiming to a disbanded audience.

Before we opened the car doors, we were told that what we were about to see was unique and of great value. My mother's skeptical brows rose eloquently. The house looked hardly more than a shack in the middle of nowhere. Inside, the ceilings hung low over even my short head.

The tiny lady, gracious in her smile and visibly proud of the effect on us her cottage would produce, invited us to wander around. To me, the rooms of the higgledy-piggledy house and its tiny resident belonged in a fairy tale. Above table-height, barely a square inch of wall in the four or five small chambers was left uncovered. Painting upon painting, most about the size of a school copybook turned on its side, clamoured in vibrant palette and textured topography around the confined space of what might have been the home of Snow White's seven dwarfs. How I wanted us to hurry on so I could take a swim at the public beach in Rawdon before the heat of the day wore off, but I couldn't resist the charm of the place or the draw of the bold strokes on the walls, or the plate of sandwiches the smiling, diminutive hostess put out on the gingham cloth of her Hobbit's table.

I understood nothing about the paintings or even the person we were introduced to as the sister of a Canadian painter. But I did understand what it was Mr. Benoit wanted us, the little family of immigrants, to take away. Something native to the place, to this place alone in all the world, that we would in time have a right to call ours. I could hear my mother thinking, "As if . . ." As if anything as valuable as the paintings of a famous artist could be patched around a shack of a cottage, unsecured by glass or alarm, open to the breeze wafting from the windows and to the dusty country air. But we saw what we saw, and eventually as a college student, I understood the extent of it. All those sketches dashed off in the bush onto small, rectangular, wooden panels that everyone can see now at the McMichael and the Art Gallery of Ontario and the National Gallery in Ottawa. "Thank you, Miss Jackson," we each pressed her hand as we left, even me the littlest one, the urban child born in Budapest to be raised in Montreal. I had spied with my little eye a distillation of landscape that spelled Country. The houses and schools and shopping centres of my recently built suburb seemed suddenly toy-like and ersatz. I had fallen hard for the 'fundament' in fundamentals.

Because my parents didn't drive, we used to get around the city by public trolley, bus, and later the subway. The only cars I rode in were those of my uncle and the parents of my friends. Their fathers drove us to lessons at the East End Boys and Girls Club on Hochelaga Street, a twenty-minute drive out of suburban Ville d'Anjou, and the mothers would rescue us from downpours at lunchtime or after school. The rain brought with it a carnival atmosphere of disrupted routine when we'd break outside in our plaid raincoats to scan the cars pulling in at a diagonal, wipers beating excitedly. I'd hold back a second, hoping one of my friends would not forget me in the tumult, but call out at the last moment: "Judy, my mom says do you want a ride?"

My uncle seemed to have a new car each year I drove up with him along the Laurentian Autoroute to the fashionable country house in St. Sauveur, built to resemble a Swiss chalet. Usually just the two of us rode up in companionable silence as my aunt and cousins had been ensconced there since the start of the summer. My uncle and I were never as comfortable together as when we didn't have to speak to each other, and without the others around, there was no pretence to keep up. We lapsed into our separate mental preoccupations, so much so that often our arrival felt premature to me, however much I'd looked forward to seeing Pauline. I overindulged in a rich inner life—fantasies of glorified achievements and romantic conquests that were so compelling—and I clung to consciousness at bedtime, just to run the scenarios over and over, reluctant to let them blend into the more pedestrian musings of dream. The drive to the country was another gateway to reverie. My uncle would think his thoughts and I mine as I stared out the window at the flat commercial terrain that held on doggedly until just a few exit ramps before our turnoff. Then, as one was just about to give up on the landscape, the mountains burst around a bend, thickly furred in cedar, maple, pine, and birch. The ancient hills rolled, one into the next, and I knew, achingly reluctant to leave my private world, and achingly glad to be here at last, that we were close.

One of the great pleasures of my childhood was sitting facing Pauline on a padded lounge chair, with a Chinese checkers board or a pack of cards between us. No one was permitted into the lake for at least an hour after lunch. We settled into a corner of the balcony that girded the house, a good distance from where my aunt had pulled her lounge chair for her postprandial nap. We whisper-bickered good-naturedly over our games. Glancing up from the cards, we'd look out over the light-pocked lake where the occasional paddle boat nodded under the midday sun. Blinding spots erased our hands momentarily when we looked back down. Doing handstands in the water, jumping off the floating dock, and water-skiing over the wakes of the motor boat my elder cousin steered expertly but without regard to our safety or comfort at the end of the tow rope, were our favourite pastimes. The aim of each day was to be in the water optimally: before lunch, afternoons, and one last dip after dinner, *Get Smart*, and *Batman*, by which time the hour of prohibition would have passed. Yet, when I look back on my summers at their country house, the idyllic moments that come back to me are the hours of playing Parcheesi on the wraparound balcony or out in the rowboat under the blazing sun, languidly, sun-sapped of energy, laying out the cards in endless lines of "War."

The last time I stayed at my aunt's country house, I was a new mother of a seven-month-old infant, drawn there by emergency. Pauline and I had drifted apart in our teens, and I had never even seen the most recent house they had built on a much grander scale than the first. I was thirty, my mother and aunt in their mid-sixties, my father, in hospital, within a couple of years of eighty. He and my mother had been visiting in St. Sauveur when he'd suffered a stroke. The distance between the village of St. Sauveur and the town of St. Jerome, where the nearest hospital is located, is only about thirty kilometres, but the house was another twenty minutes from the village by small, hilly roads. My aunt, even on her serene days, was never calm behind the wheel. Moreover, the two women were not capable of lifting a paralyzed man into my aunt's car. An ambulance had to be dispatched. All this took some time while time was of the essence. Had my father anticipated, somewhere in his country-rooted bones all that long time ago on Lac Maskinongé after which he refused to holiday with them again, that hanging out with my aunt in the country would not be good for his health? I drove from Toronto to Montreal with my baby, my late husband Craig having had to stay back to field a crisis at work. In Montreal, we picked up my sister and her two young daughters. En route to St. Jerome, the heavens unleashed a storm. Rain pelted down, instantly flooding the highway and turning it, as Lac Maskinongé was once turned, aroil. All visibility washed out. Our car of females and an infant crept to an overpass. We listened to the rain pound overhead. No one spoke. It felt apocalyptic. My father would take another six years to die, but it was clear this was it, the paterfamilias cut down.

My infant son had a gluttonous appetite, capable of nursing for hours. At my aunt's, exhausted after the strain of the drive and the shock of seeing my father stripped of speech, I kept the baby in bed with me so I might at least try to sleep through his feeds. A thin, early light seeped through the blinds as I startled awake. There were shouts. Panicked footsteps raced around the too many large rooms. My aunt started to scream. In French, she invoked death upon something or other. In Hungarian, she keened, "Eaten. He's been eaten!" My door burst open. I had never seen my mother this wild, not even when she had recounted how one of her sisters had died during a bombardment. This was when a relative who had been recently discovered to be living in New York, had visited for the first time. I was ten years old again, frozen to the spot as her voice lurched to a pitiful pitch. She had completely lost anchor. "Where is the baby?" she shrieked in Hungarian. "The baby. The baby! The dog ate the baby!" My aunt had a German shepherd called Brutus, whom she pampered and adored. Having survived Auschwitz and Buchenwald, she had taken in a German shepherd rescue dog. The bigness of my aunt's heart, so big, so generous, so nuts. Hearing the horror articulated, she too filled my doorway, her face all expression, no sound. It was like waking up to an Eisenstein movie. I pulled back the covers to reveal my son, latched on as always, not the least disturbed by the commotion nor distracted from his purpose. I was to learn that when my mother had woken, she'd poked her head into my room. I can't really say why except she has always had a penchant for breaching personal space. Not seeing the baby, she'd leapt to the obvious conclusion.

* * *

I won't say I married my husband Craig because his family had been here for generations or because on his mother's side they'd held rural property. "Correction," Craig would have said, "a farm." Not a prosperous one, given that it turned a stone-packed soil, the stone fences of cleared fields a reminder of an original mineral more than forested profusion. The fact of land in the country appealed where reason left off, and was hard for me to let go of once the farm was sold to pay for a retirement bungalow. Craig hadn't felt the call to look it up on any of our vacations to the beach in its vicinity. As a boy, he had holidayed at the farm each summer. It was the beach he had loved and the beach to which we returned as a young couple and then with our children. The fact that his own parents, like us, rented a different cottage at this beach every year, perpetually nomadic in our quest for the one with the best location, least mould, and most tolerable mattresses—weighing these odds to come up with the annual lacklustre compromise—was plainly wrong. Craig's maternal ancestors had lived here for generations, owned land here, and cleared it of the dolomite and sandstone and shale that stood in the way of accessing the necessities of life. This, only for our generation to arrive landless, sans tenure, supplicant in this very place for a roof over our heads. Craig accepted the twist of fate without resentment, but I felt cheated of the claim to land that had called to me in the form of a generous-spirited, large-boned young man of country stock.

During our first months under one roof, my second husband, John, took me to Budapest to reintroduce me to the city of my birth. He had worked in Budapest in a consulting capacity for a number of years. There is a photo of me standing under the sign that reads Obstetrics in the hospital where my mother had given birth fifty years before. We'd walked the same blocks she had in the middle of a January squall, from my family's flat on Rona *Útça*. Just a half hour earlier, John had passed me his cellphone to dial her in Montreal. I said, "Mummy, I'm looking up at our flat on the second floor. The daughter-in-law of the lady below, the same lady who's lived here all these years but is in hospital now, the daughter-in-law won't buzz us in to let us look around. I'm standing here on the outside of the fence, Ma." An ocean between us, I start to blubber. My mother, over the same impossible distance, arrives as by Star Trek transporter, her disembodied self fully manifest in a slurry of Hungarian maledictions. Her wicked tongue is a balm. Though my words, "here, on the outside of the fence," opened an old wound of displacement, she understands them on another level: that she, as in through one of hers, has been denied. She would give that dirty so-and-so of a daughter-in-law a piece of her mind if we put the cellphone to the intercom. Instead, she settled for instructing John. "I walked to the hospital on my own feet, leaning on our cleaning lady, because Judy's father was outside the city at his job with the state farms. I had the pains. The snow was coming at us sideways, it was so windy. Where would we get a taxi? You take her now. She will walk like I did to the place she was born. But she will have you."

John also took me into the region of the Hungarian countryside dotted with the erstwhile agricultural estates of my father's large, dispossessed family. He showed me where he thought my grandparents' house would have stood, by some bricks half-buried in a plausible depression. I dug one out. With my bare hands, I scraped up a fistful of earth that I poured into a baggy that held my daily dose of vitamin supplements. The elderly cousin of my father, who had accompanied us as a guide, pointed out the pine trees my murdered grandmother had planted as a young bride just before the turn of the twentieth century. They were now over a hundred years in that ground. I peeled a piece of bark from one of them and picked three pine cones to stash in my purse. These bits and shards of a broken past sit on my bookshelf today. Sometimes I look at the dirt preserved in a spice jar or pick up the old brick. I'm afraid the bark or the pine cones might crumble at touch. I may dream all I want of owning a cottage in the country, but no piece of Canadian wilderness, however artfully presented, could replace what history gutted.

Hindsight Comes
Too Late

WHEN MY FATHER OPENS the front door on a sight that floors him, it is 1969 and I'm fifteen, and he is sixty-three. Our half of the duplex contains two units and a separate entry basement that serves primarily as our TV room. It also shelters—to a point—the piano I abuse for forty-five minutes daily. I would become more proficient at gauging the exact amount of time that elapsed in my practice period than I would playing Scarlatti sonatinas and ever more tiresome scales. As a result, fifty years on, I still gloat about my unerring sense of time, while another piano sits in dumb reproof against my kitchen wall. In the far corner of my childhood basement, behind my sullen back at the piano stool, is the stolid walnut desk purchased for my father at a fusty-smelling used furniture store on Ontario Street East. For the ten-year-old accompanying her mother on the birthday present–buying expedition, there was a sense of slumming it outside the crisp boundaries of our new development. It seemed somewhat of a back-handed gift to offer my father a used desk to put into our contemporary faux-wood-panelled rec room. Of course, the bona fide solidity was exactly what my mother was looking for at a price we could afford. At least, I begged, already honing a Montrealer's eye for chic, no curlicues even if they would remind Daddy of the Victorian furnishings he'd grown up with in rural Hungary. As a result, the desk we chose was too nondescript to boast any style. It suited my father's pared-down expectations.

My mother and I used the basement more than he did, watching television every evening, and for my odious piano regime after school, but he made an occasion of going downstairs on the weekends to write long airmail letters to friends and family abroad. He'd declare he was on his way down and to whom he'd be writing, and there was a sense of consequence about the matter, as though he were about to commune with royalty. In April, though, the desk took on a burden of activity that papered its usually bare surface with the documents of my parents' tax returns. To my father, all government officials were equally suspect, requiring utmost care in one's dealings with them, a legacy of the anti-Jewish measures during the years leading to the war, compounded by worse that followed.

Though born in Budapest, I was very much a North American girl who showed up, a stranger in my birthplace, in the summer of '69 wearing skirts so short I couldn't raise my arm to the overhead bar of the bus we took from my father's aged auntie's apartment to the government-run handicraft outlets on downtown Váci *Útca*. I would much rather have been home in Montreal listening to the soundtrack of Hair, and Steppenwolf reminding me I was never destined for dour, Soviet repression but rather "Born to Be Wild."

Unbeknownst to my parents, I had, that spring, exercised this birthright by showing up on the street where a boy I liked lived. My girlfriend Cerise and I found him playing street hockey like a kid in front of the address we'd looked up in the phone book. It was a bold move for a girl who had been taught to be prim, inaccessible, but ultimately receptive. According to my mother, the man takes and the woman gives, the sum total of her imparted wisdom on male-female relations. We all knew without being told that nice girls, at least up until our time, didn't put out.

It's a few days after I personally delivered my message of availability to the boy two bus rides away. My father doesn't at first believe what his senses have told him as he shuts the door, turning the clip on the doorknob for emphasis. At least the slide of the dead bolt has not reinforced the insult. "Who was that?" my mother calls from the kitchen, while I charge out of my bedroom yelling, "Is someone at the door?" My father stands in the hall, arms hanging helplessly, and with an almost puppyish raising of his thick, patrician brows. After some inarticulate mouthing, "I don't know," is his bewildering reply. It should be noted that in our household, everybody always knows everything. Even I, the youngest, who is no longer the littlest but still treated as such, uses a tone of informed certainty. My father is a generous person who keeps peppermints in his pockets to hand out to the neighbouring children as he shovels the walk or mows the lawn. He sends money to Israel and to the relatives behind the Iron Curtain. His old-fashioned manners make him courteous to a fault, according to my mother, especially when he invites the plumber to sit down to a cup of tea in the living room, no less, much to the tradesman's discomfort. So it is unclear whether his reply, "I don't know," refers to himself, as in, he doesn't know who he is by this act of rudeness, or if it applies to the discreet taps continuing from the stairwell.

I fling the door open on the tall, absurdly skinny reed I had outrageously invited over. My mother wipes her hands in her apron, trying on a few expressions, not immediately finding one to suit the occasion, while my father fails to reach into his pocket for a peppermint, though his hand has gravitated there by habit. Taking advantage of the undreamed-of luck provided by the pause, I lead the boy into my room.

* * *

My sister, wedded at age twenty, was in the third quarter of her first year of marriage when the boy who became my first boyfriend knocked at our door. In fact, my sister's courtship had lasted five years, so she, too, had been fifteen when a boy first came calling. A kid who was by nature a pest, I'd been easily enlisted to tail the two teenagers on their flight to the school grounds where ostensibly the boy was to teach my sister to hit a tennis ball against a wall. I don't think my parents considered her chastity seriously in peril; it was propriety they hoped to maintain.

The fights I remember that came later as marriage hove into view were about my sister's boyfriend not being Jewish, and if my parents wished to push their point, they'd harp on his poor social graces, not that he was crass, but he was practically mute compared to our crowd that ran at the mouth—well, compared to anybody. I don't remember my father having meltdowns about my sister becoming a woman, a term of the day. I may have been the youngest, privileging my status in the affections of the male parent, but there was no objective reason to believe that my father in any way loved me more.

Yet the violent emotion he brought to my coming into my sexuality was, I think, out of proportion to the provocation. My sister had 'visited' with her boyfriend in that same bedroom, also with the door open. Even I didn't have the nerve to shut it. I don't recall my father patrolling the hall outside her room like a pacing Rottweiler the way he did while my boyfriend and I tried to get in some necking. As his feet approached, we bolted upright; when they reluctantly passed, we sank back onto the still warm bedspread. Needless to say, the interruptions only heightened the charge between us. It would have served my father right, I thought, if he'd felt a shock while lingering in the open socket of the threshold, not quite able to barge in.

I suspect he harboured the hope that a family trip to Europe that summer would be long enough—six weeks—to nip the fledgling rela-tionship in the bud. As absence does, it intensified my longing. The hard-earned dollars spent on ferrying me over the ocean clearly had been wasted. In London, in Paris, in Vienna, the only site I was interested in checking out was the central post office where a letter might be waiting in care of General Delivery. Either way, I'd languish in the hotel room all afternoon, mourning if I had received nothing, deep in a many-paged response if I had. By the time we reached Budapest, my father must have run out of patience.

Here's the nub. The question of patience. Not a word weighted with emotion, yet it's taken 1,500 of them here before I could lay it down in print. A word that makes me want to snatch it back, as if revoking the word is all it would take to spare us. From my earliest memories and the time the English language grew in my mouth, I would have described my father first as a patient man. Not a Jewish, Hungarian, immigrant, or Holocaust-surviving man, or family-loving, elderly, or story-telling man. He was a man of great patience. He needed to be to keep the peace with my quick-to-ignite, quick-to-judge-or-condemn mother and his two quarrelsome daughters. Yet, that summer, unwittingly and unintentionally, I tried my father's patience.

The pantheon of my father's weekend correspondents included three lifelong friends, in fact, the only friends I knew my father to have outside his family both in Canada and abroad. He had met all three at the Academy of Agronomy in the city of Debrecen during the period of *numerus clausus* that had targeted Jews in the 1920s, making Hungary cutting edge, as it were, in the enactment of European anti-Semitism between the wars. Wili *bácsi*, Laci *bácsi*, Zoli *bácsi*, and their wives were in the crowd greeting our train when it pulled in at Budapest's *Keletipája Udvar*. In our twelve years in Canada, my family of four had not acquired a combined circle of acquaintance equal to my father's surviving kin and connections gathered on the station platform. The fifteen-year-old looked sideways at her old, plodding, usually out-of-place sire, seeing him for a brief moment as he might have looked in a sepia-coloured print with a bemedaled sash across his chest. During our two weeks in Budapest, his dance card was full from morning to night, a perpetual round of invitations to four-course meals and endless cups of *'preszo* served with slices of *dobos torta*. Among his brethren, I became known as the pretty daughter and my married sister the charming one. Unlike my sister, who has always garnered compliments, this was the one time in my life I enjoyed attention for my round-cheeked looks. The swap for me from nice and charming to pretty was an easy trade.

I had been raised on stories of the exemplary natures of my father, his two brothers who died during the war, and the three friends of the station platform. In my mind, picturing them on a Hollywood set, they were cast less as the *bácsis*, or uncles, and more as the six Magyar amigos.

I imagined five more or less similar versions of my patient, honourable father, all wearing felt fedoras. Zoli *bácsi* was the closest match, Laci *bácsi*, a somewhat irritable second, and Wili *bácsi*, a bombastic spouter of pronouncements, who made my family of know-it-alls seem amateurs by comparison. My father loved this man? Wili *bácsi* was my first exposure to someone who had been on the receiving end of vicious persecution, and then turned the same weapon against another racialized group. This became apparent as he opined on the race riots that had taken place in US cities in the last years. Had he read about these riots in the not-so-objective state press? I not-so-innocently asked. My father shot me a look. Undaunted, I persisted. How many Blacks had Wili *bácsi* made the acquaintance of? One thing led to another until I burst out that, of course, I would marry a Black man if we loved each other.

"Marry a Black man, preposterous," my father muttered on our way back to the aged auntie's.

"Why not? Why shouldn't I if he were the kind of good, decent person, a man like you, say, and I loved him?"

"Why shouldn't? Why shouldn't? Have you lost your mind?"

Who was this Wili *bácsi* that he could be such a bad influence on my father?

"Never," he seethed, "have I been so mortified!"

"What, not even when that anti-Semite at the Academy slapped you in the face?"

I had such confidence in my father's doting love, such faith in my knowledge of his patient, giving character, such reliance on his intelligent appreciation of my wit. My mother told me to shut up before my father had a stroke. And yes, for the first time I saw something in his face I didn't recognize, a ripple below the surface of, simply, someone else.

* * *

Few visitors to Budapest pass up an excursion to Gellért Hill from which, on the Buda side of the Danube, one is treated to panoramic views of both Pest and Buda. By the time we had climbed past couples making out on benches, admired the vistas, and descended, my feet, which I had found fetching that morning in the slingback heels I insisted on wearing because they were the best complement to my mini dress, throbbed. I took the pumps off on the Liberty Bridge, insouciantly swinging them from their straps as we crossed back over the famous river.

"Put them on, now," my father hissed behind me in the heavily accented English he'd left behind on the Orient Express. I swerved to respond while continuing backwards, a saucy move I assumed would prove irresistible. "You'd rather my feet start bleeding just because of what a bunch of strangers might think?"

He said nothing at first but then surged by me, sputtering, "Fine, you can walk by yourself, but I won't be seen with you."

My father loved being seen with his three well-dressed females, but he would repudiate me once more on this holiday when in Vienna my mother and I had a little too much of the young, un-aged summer wine served up in a beer hall. Rarely compatible, we tripped along, inclining our heads towards each other, tittering as we skirted a car coming at us on the street. "Disgusting," my father shuddered, "nothing but a pair of drunken women." It would turn out that when my father referred to me as a woman, he meant nothing good by it.

My father and his two younger brothers came of age on an affluent country estate that relied on the work of Hungarian peasants. After the boys reached puberty, they were given a discreet outbuilding to which they might withdraw to satisfy their manly needs. This included 'entertaining,' by which today we would mean exploiting peasant girls who lived with their families and consequently were also employed on the property. My father described the difference in character between Feri, his next-in-age brother, and himself in this way: whereas my father had his preferred girl and 'stayed true to her,' his brother said he didn't like to have a girl hang around him long enough to start to smell or perhaps to leave her scent on him. I can't remember which, and it hardly matters since both are regrettable. As a young person, I forgave my father's behaviour given its cultural context and viewed it as another example of his gentle side. Now I deem it only marginally better than his brother's. He did not condemn Feri *bácsi*. He had merely alluded to their differences. He may even have given a little humorous snort as he said it.

When I was an angry girl of seventeen who dropped out of high school, I eventually got a job with a Hungarian man who, like my parents, was a refugee of the 1956 revolution. He ran a small business of buying eyeglass frames from wholesalers and distributing them to opticians and optometrists. I was his stockroom clerk and sole full-time employee. When business picked up, he would hire a sales rep on an as-need basis. Because we spent hours in each other's company with little to do, I heard more than was necessary of his past. He told me about following a beautiful woman who had given him the eye back in Budapest before the war. He described her in elaborate detail, her glossy hair under a wool beret, plaid coat, rust-red low-heeled shoes, her doe-like legs, and so on. Into a stairwell he'd eagerly pursued her, but once clinched together behind closed doors, he was overcome by a powerful odour. Her sex, he said, stank of corruption.

I recoiled, literally feeling struck by the misogynistic mouthful. Wasn't the telling of this anecdote to a seventeen-year-old girl not as offensive in its way as the conflicted description itself? I knew my boss was fond of me in a fatherly and not-so-fatherly way. I felt as though he had jumped at me from across his desk which, months later, he did.

The bad smell raised by my uncle and my boss summed up how Hungarian men of my father's generation regarded women. A sampling too minuscule to be meaningful, but it was reinforced by others in my parents' circle, by the change in their behaviours once their daughters and their friends were old enough to attract boys. Good fathers turned into crazed knights championing their womenfolk's honour. Funny, facetious *bácsis* made passes at girls who just a year or so ago they had chauffeured to amusement parks and innocently treated to cotton candy. Humbert Humberts one and all, for whom a girl turned woman, a girl hanging around long enough to become a woman, a woman, in other words, was a girl gone bad in an over-ripened sense, inherently spoiled.

* * *

Two things changed in me towards the boy over the eleven months we were together. The more 'into' him I got—the more obsessive, if you would, my attachment—the less responsive I became when we made out. I don't remember this as a sudden change, but one that crept over me, not unlike the metamorphosis overtaking my father. Did I notice that sometimes his naps were longer than usual on weekends, or that he stayed home from work once in a while so he could sleep most of the day? If I did, it didn't register. My father was older than anybody else's dad and different in many ways. Every so often over the years before I left home, my mother would say, "Your father had another spell yesterday." He had taken to passing out in the street occasionally, often enough to warrant the word 'another.' Afterwards, he'd have a much longer than usual sleep. He never appeared injured following these attacks and resumed his activities as before.

Did I make much of it? The question is rather, did these spells concern me an iota? I didn't even worry when my parents, who had learned to drive too late, my mother in her fifties and my father over sixty, had an accident that mercifully totalled the weapon they had taken on the road. They were okay? Fine then, and on I went with my own preoccupations. Even at nineteen, in college and living independently, I had yet to attain much discernible empathy for those who had raised me. My father had prostate surgery at the time, and all I recall feeling was chagrin at having to waste my precious time visiting him in hospital. It took me almost five decades to excuse my father, dead now a quarter century, for being human. I can only conjecture that in some regards, my young heart had gone numb.

Apparently not the only part. What could have induced me to take the boy down to the basement? Perhaps desperation. I was desperate for my switch to flip back on. I was desperate to stay in love, to be in love, desperate for love not to end. And why so desperate at age sixteen? He should have been just the first of a long line, like the boys fluttering like streamers from the beautiful kite who was my friend Cerise. Why could I not accept that the boy who had played coy when I initially got hot and heavy was a boy ill-suited to my needs and that I'd best move on? Instead, I clung more tightly while the last spark of desire fizzled out.

There was a flip-open sofa bed in the basement. My mother would stretch out on it to watch the movie of the week. The couch must have been already open. Perhaps Cerise had spent the night, and after being up most of the wee hours dancing to and acting out Jesus Christ Superstar, I hadn't gotten around to putting the basement back in order. Perhaps that's what gave me the idea. A desperate measure. I took the boy downstairs so we could neck in peace.

Instead, I suffered. Try as we might, I no longer felt anything in my body while my heart yet longed for this boy. Upstairs, my father started to go crazy. Why should this have taken me by surprise? On what planet had I taken up residence? My father's irascibility had become a regular feature in his relations with all of us. Apparently, no one provokes as flagrantly as a child who has detected parental blood in the waters but refuses to accept her father might be at risk of going under. I'd repaired to the basement to be with my boyfriend behind closed doors. His daughter. A daughter of the sacrosanct lineage sacrificed on the pyre of brutality. Daring openly to besmirch herself. There was a very bad scene. My father spat words I had never heard from him about anyone. He went so far as to raise a fist. Stunned, all I could think of was the searing injustice, as I hadn't enjoyed a moment of the unconsummated transgression.

Throughout my childhood, my father used to tell me that I was capable of becoming anything. How much had idealization on both our parts infused our love? Were we not destined both to fall? I fell for an unripe boy just at the moment that my father began to change from the indulgent parent I had adored to a man confounded by his mortality. I took all my delicate eggs, transferred them to a very flimsy basket, then couldn't figure out why so many broke.

Trans-Canada

PSYCHOLOGICAL COLLAPSE, like a flat tire or a snapped fan belt, used to be referred to as a breakdown. After an adjustment of sorts, the damaged individual returned to the road. 'Nervous' breakdown seemed more like a tizzy. My aunt, we heard, had 'broken down' during a roll call in the concentration camp, inciting a *kapo*, a prisoner-overseer, to render her eye into seeping mucilage I pictured oozing down her cheek like raw egg. My auntie's provocation had been in mentally vacating the body that had stood for hours in the sun, allowing her mouth to fall open in a silent grimace. According to my pragmatic mother, the pre-emptive beating saved her sister's life. She'd had a second breakdown, we learned, in the furnace of the Israeli desert where my uncle sent her after the war. He claimed that settlement in *Ha'aretz* or conversion to Christianity were their only options as persecuted Jews, so she'd better test out what living as a pioneer would be like. In this case, too, my aunt's protest by taking leave of her senses seemed eminently sane to me. A generous mother, consummate cook, and expert saleswoman, there was nothing in her makeup to lead me to find her mentally defective. The mentally deranged had to be contained in fortresses like Saint-Jean-de-Dieu, which entered our lives after the opening in 1963 of Place Versailles, the first indoor shopping mall in Montreal. Saint-Jean-de-Dieu was located on Sherbrooke Street across from the mall and almost kitty-corner to Dunton High School. Giddily cutting class to rifle through the record stacks of Miracle Mart, we'd caution each other about acting obviously high and ending up among the loonies in Saint-Jean-des-Fous. The mentally *ill* existed in the abstract, notwithstanding the edifice's looming presence.

My teacher in grade five, Mrs. Bruce, was unusually devoted to the enlightenment of her students. It was not until she reverted to her maiden name, Roy, a few years later, missing months of school to an undisclosed ailment, that I understood her dedication had bordered on pathological. Until that rough patch, I'd considered Mrs. Bruce to be the most dynamic teacher one could have. During these troubles, my mother occasionally got a call from her colleague who was obviously not too sick to pick up the phone. After their whispered conversation, my mother would hang up sighing in Hungarian, "Poor woman." Discounting my parents who both bore scars from the war, my father's teeth-gnashing over Canadian snowstorms, my mother's hair-trigger panic when something went wrong with a household appliance, Miss Roy's malaise was my first encounter with mental disorder. In fact, the transformation of the fervent teacher into someone totally incapable of entering a classroom could not have been more clearly laid out than by her demotion from Mrs. to Miss. The undoing of Mrs. Bruce into Miss Roy was an object lesson I was meant to read loud and clear, my mother's whispers to the contrary.

Because she'd been my favourite teacher, I felt some right to know the details of Miss Roy's undoing. My mother did not keep confidences to herself. She often shared staff room gossip at dinner: "But don't you dare say anything!" The ghastly past, too, was on panoramic display on a regular basis. Suddenly something about the reverse transubstantiation of Mrs. Bruce into someone frighteningly diminished was not a topic for a child of good family.

The Mrs. Bruce I had known was a middle-aged lady with tight curls, broad hips clad in rusty tartan or the grey wool of a warden. My grade-four teacher, Miss Kerner, had been slender and chic; in grade three, Miss Yasukawa had charmed us with her petite, soft-spoken ways. Mrs. Bruce, standing sentinel in the grade-five doorway on the first day of school, filled us with foreboding as we slunk past without the usual charge at claiming our desks. Soon it was clear she adored children. She seemed to love us before learning our thirty-odd names. It showed in her eager rolling down of the map for the first time, as though only the choicest children deserved such a privilege. Her passion was geography. She taught us each subject by way of the map.

Maps and I were old familiars. In our basement, taped to the wood laminate wall, was a map of the filleted world dominated by its blue oceans, its nations set off in candy-necklace colours. I tried to lure my friends into contests using the map, but they lost interest when they saw how practiced I was. During the bright summer months, I spent hours in the dim coolness, testing myself with the location of towns, cities, and countries, many of which I'd heard mentioned by my parents and the few relatives recovered from the lost past, now living in New York, Boston, and Philadelphia. Their talk of foreign parts included tales of daring escape. I scoured the maps of Europe, South America, and the United States, thrilled when a familiar name popped out like Livingstone in the jungle.

Mrs. Bruce introduced me to the map of Canada, the dimensions of which were so large, I started to understand how much country stretched beyond our dot of Montreal. All trajectories in family lore came from the east and the south, so my eye had found little incentive to stray westward. The map, which Mrs. Bruce found any excuse during any subject to roll down and tap with a pointer, covered most of the front blackboard. The world in my basement would have fit into it three times over. The map was a thing of beauty rendered three-dimensionally in brown and white-capped elevations, green forests, beige tundras, and myriads of blue pools and rivers. I don't think it included roads, but I have no doubt that the train routes across the country, instrumental in binding its regions into a federation, would have appeared as lovely cross-hatched threads joining sea to sea. Mrs. Bruce waxed rhapsodically about the train's flying saucer-like dome car offering 360-degree views of the Rockies, and its riverbank-hugging gyrations through their canyons. But her favourite ribbon of transport, too new to appear on a map of school board issue, was the recently opened Trans-Canada Highway. It seemed as nascent as our suburb of vacant lots, inching ever longer like a child against a growth chart. In 1964, the Trans-Canada had been operational for two years but would not be completed for another seven. By that time, the sad story of Miss Roy would have played out. I have no way of knowing if she recovered from her breakdown to climb back into her Rambler to drive the full, 8,000 kilometres from St. John's, Newfoundland, to Victoria, British Columbia. This would have been for her an apotheosis of sorts. As it was, she extolled the open road, the deep pleasures and educational properties of the road trip, and the automobile as the great freedom machine of the everyman-and-woman. I recall her wonder about visiting the famous reversing falls in New Brunswick (and, way over on the other side of the map on another trip, the great redwood she once tunnelled through in her Rambler). When as a class we were well-behaved and caught up on our work, she rewarded us by dividing us into teams like other classes did for spelling bees, rolled down the great map of Canada, and set us to locating lakes, rivers, islands, straits, cities, towns, and capitals, convinced she was imparting basic training for life.

* * *

I was sixteen when my parents, on the advice of my father's cousin Zsuzsa, sent me to the psychiatric clinic at the Montreal Children's Hospital. I'd stopped playing guitar. I refused to join the family for dinner. Instead of doing homework, I sat hunched on the floor over my portable Singer, sewing long dresses with folk motifs and flowing tops made of cast-off curtains and throws. These I would wear to folk music venues known as coffee houses and return from downtown smelling of cigarettes and something more pungent. Perhaps they panicked when I made noises about dropping out of my last year; until the first report card that October, I'd placed top in my grade.

Six months previously, I had been jilted. Zsuzsa lived across the border. She had a daughter my age with whom I was close. I was sent to them to be disabused of my fixation. They explained that what I felt couldn't be love, but rather an emotion more like obsession and what would become an ugly word during the freedom-worship of the seventies—dependence.

"Tell that to Natalie!" I raged. Not having been privy to the particulars of Miss Roy's breakdown nor to my aunt's crises of commitment to life and faith, I'd come to rely on fiction to walk me through the descending steps of opting out when the terms proved unacceptable. Much of my sentimental education came from the movies once a week on Academy Performance. Our rabbit ears brought in four channels, two of them English and two French. This meant we watched only the English CBC and CTV, which aired some American broadcasts. Academy Performance featured many of the movies my mother had watched with Hungarian subtitles before the war: Vivien Leigh in *Gone with the Wind* and Greta Garbo in *Ninotchka*. But more recent productions came to us, too, on Saturday nights: *To Kill a Mockingbird* and *Cleopatra*. *The Great Escape* and *Judgement at Nuremberg* were the only films lacking a female lead that my mother watched through to the end. Even Gregory Peck, her heartthrob, failed to bring the screen to life without a female foil. Before dismissing *Moby Dick* with twirl of the knob, she sniffed, "It's a crime to disfigure such a face with a Methuselah beard. *Fuj*! [Hungarian expletive of disgust]." I was eleven when we watched Warren Beatty break Natalie Wood's heart in *Splendor in the Grass*. The injustice of her treatment by Beatty's father, and her boyfriend's betrayal of their great love reduced me to a sopping mess, while my mother sighed over the tragedy of Natalie's wasted looks, "All her future before her," meaning the currency of her beauty poured down the drain. I was outraged that Natalie's breakdown wasn't compensated as it should have been for pain unfairly inflicted. Instead, she was punishingly incarcerated with the mad. Breakdowns like hers were due to rational forces. The correct realignment of circumstances would have been an obvious fix.

Just around the time my mother and I watched *Splendor in the Grass*, we were walking to catch the bus that would take us to the mall. By way of welcoming spring, I had pulled an outfit out of camphor-laced storage—a navy-blue swing coat with large buttons, white gloves, and a white peaked go-go hat. My mother wore gloves with her coral twill. I sensed her approval of my ensemble. It buoyed my confidence. For once, my appearance reflected well on her. We were mutually gratified for the moment, and I felt a rare impulse to give her something. I said, "I know what I'm going to be when I grow up. I'm going to marry a man with lots and lots of degrees." By which I meant someone brilliant whose degrees earned millions, thus satisfying us both. Naturally, my mother laughed. She didn't say rich would be enough, or that "being" something was not the same as who one marries. She didn't need to correct me because as far as she was concerned, there was nothing wrong with the spirit of my ambition. She laughed because I'd pleased her. When my boyfriend left me a few years later, I'd already concluded what a girl was worth without a man. I watched my future gurgle down the drain that had swallowed Natalie's looks.

For almost fifty years, I've kept a reminder on the premises of how beside myself, as in departed from self, I once shifted. I still have my song sheets slashed with black magic marker. A sign in orange construction paper on my bedroom door warned all who approached to FUCK OFF! (I warmed to the point of a temporary thaw hearing my shrill mother beg prettily about guests coming to dinner.) My ferocity scared us all. I had been an obedient child, good student, sufficiently demure with men to reassure my mother that her example had rubbed off. What was this unravelling over a mere boy?

"The Children's" is located on the western edge of downtown. I took the usual bus and subway to cross the city, more than an hour. If my parents had offered to accompany me, I had probably rebuffed them. I meant to reflect the gravity of a woman spurned. I took a seat on a bench in the hallway. I'd come after school wearing my navy-blue, V-necked tunic. We had waged war against the dress code, advancing as far as to be excused from the regulation white blouse and dark knee socks. The hold-over tunic represented the last gasp of cursed regimentation. I wore a raspberry-coloured shirt underneath, with matching braided headband and peace symbol necklace to indicate contempt for convention. The minutes of sitting on the bench stretched into two hours, bringing back the humiliation of those made to stand outside the principal's office in grade school. The longer I sat, the more self-conscious and guilty I felt, forced to contemplate my deficits.

The doctor was tall, athletic, with the kind of watery-brown hair that might have started out ginger. He bunched up his sleeves behind his desk. Why, he launched, had my parents sent me? Did I take drugs? Did I sleep around? My mind cast about the various girlfriends' bedrooms, as well as our basement pull-out couch where Cerise and I spent many an overnight gossiping and solving the woes of the world. "You know what I'm talking about, boys, men, sex. Have you had sex?" "Yes?" I answered. "With how many?" I stared. "I know you kids. Do you at least use a condom?" I shrivelled to a nub. All that making out on my girlhood bed, which I'd considered the intimate glory called making love, disqualified. A depressed child when I'd entered his office, I reeled out wiser. My behaviour seemed aberrant to my old-world parents, but it didn't raise an eyebrow of social perception. Within the month, I left school.

Thirty years later, my husband Craig would sit beside me in an office in the psychiatric wing of a Toronto research hospital. The ward physicians rotated every eight weeks. This one was a tall redhead, in his forties, like us. He exuded a physical enthusiasm for the challenge that sat defeated opposite him. He pushed aside the notes on his desk, eager to make his mark. Craig, too, was tall, athletic. He, too, had been robust. The doctor's assertive health rubbed like salt in our mutual wound. Craig's descent into madness had expunged all but our immediate painful moments. Still, something vaguely familiar about this doctor made me want to run.

Not a day of the twenty-five years Craig and I spent together did I not ask myself what I was doing there. Even on the better days, as we pushed the stroller along the boardwalk on Lake Ontario, sun gracing water and park, I'd say to myself, look, all is well. The stroller bumped rhythmically over the slats rocking our first child in his sleep. Craig's voice, all enthusiastic verve, ran through one bold business move after another. I gazed besotted at our sleeping cherub, his father's excited plans filling the space that as often as not felt like lack, and reassured myself, see, I'd been right after all. People may marry for the wrong reasons, but the marriage could work. I used to say I had fallen backwards in love with Craig. On bad days I thought, what, like into a trap? I meant I had never held him in my sights. He was a friend I didn't consider as a romantic partner until he laid out the proposition as he would his future professional projects, a good idea he set himself to sell to his CEO and, in our case, to me, the targeted market. I let myself be talked into it because, well, he was good at selling ideas. It was good in many ways.

Compatibility thrived on the ground left fallow by Eros. I admired Craig's reserves of courage against a deep lack of confidence, chronic self-derision, and an anxiety so wracking it was a wonder he could raise his head in the morning. Because these conditions were familiar, I deemed them outside the purview of pathology. I loved his talents, his uprightness, his committed work ethic, his tenderness with little children, not just his own. So much to honour, perhaps a 'realer' more substantive love, I sold myself, than the romantic sort. This narrative would have sustained me had his sensitivities not taken a virulent bent. It grieves me to remember the wrong reasons. I remained Craig's stalwart advocate until the end, but my wrong reasons wronged him.

Some years after Craig took his life, I met the man who as a boy had broken my heart. It was shocking not to know him, but more so not to recognize the voice I used to talk to for hours on end, tying up the single phone line while fending off my mother's thuds on my door. He said I, too, had changed. I laughed. "No," he said, "I'd know you even without the long hair. But I would never have expected this." He gestured with his head, taking in my typical Toronto two storey. It was a decent neighbourhood, but my children went to better schools outside our ward. "I wouldn't have guessed you'd end up so . . . settled? You were the firebrand. I got all my radical views from you. You weren't afraid of anything—your parents, the school system. You crossed them all." His turn to laugh. "I guess between us, it's you who became, well—" He was thinking the b-word—that I'd sold out.

This was puzzling. Had I ever been anything but bourgeois? A professor once called me a throwback to my parents' generation, I, who saw myself as quintessentially a child of the seventies. Defiance for me was inextricably tied to breakdown and loss. Putting my pieces back together, I'd reverted to a template after all.

When I was a heartsick teenager, had I ever thought of Mrs. Bruce as I felt my way through the dark? Probably not, although she and Natalie Wood were preserved in my makeup, stark examples of what happens when you lose your man. Like my grade-five teacher, I morphed into someone who could barely summon the will to brush her teeth. I dropped twenty pounds, gained forty, lost them all again. I lived on coffee and hard green apples. I went to the public library on Sherbrooke and Aylmer, read three pages, and then hopped on the bus again. I'd met an older boy who had his own apartment in the student ghetto around McGill University. He claimed to own a gun, which won me right over. He'd gathered a harem of which I became an unsatisfactory member when pronounced frigid. It's true, I didn't feel anything as we messed around on his discoloured sheets, still sans penetration. I continued to pine for my lost love who had grown his hair long, bought an army surplus greatcoat, and looked so cool my brittle heart cracked like a wishbone whenever I saw him. I was sent on indefinite leave to the relatives across the border who promptly returned me, defective merchandise. I might corrupt my cousin who was sleeping with her boyfriend in her mother Zsuzsa's double bed. What ailed me was not a threat to social morals evidently; rather, more like a contagion. Was nervous breakdown, contracted from unrequited love, an illness then? My parents kept sending me away for the cure. A former colleague of my mother had been my piano and guitar teacher before moving to San Francisco. It was 1971. Haight-Ashbury had declined into a skid row for drug addicts, but there was action on the steps of Ghirardelli Square.

Bongos, beads, fringes, hip-hugger jeans. Miserably, I forced myself to return to those steps because that's where it was supposed to be *at*. Did I think of Mrs. Bruce in her tartan skirt as I blew along the beach in Golden Gate Park, sand scraping my teeth? Stolid, frumpy, middle-aged lady, what could she and I have had in common besides a naive love of maps? Despite being just around the corner from her giant sequoia, I felt none of the exhilaration of travel she had promised but only a profound dislocation of self.

* * *

The book my friends and I were reading while I finished high school at mind-numbing night school was Alice Munro's *Lives of Girls and Women*. Perhaps because she wrote as a Canadian and we were, obviously, Canadian girls, it touched us more nearly than Doris Lessing's *Children of Violence* had in high school, or than *The Golden Notebook* and *The Second Sex* would. Because of Alice Munro, we started to call ourselves feminists.

* * *

I spent the two summers flanking my university-qualifying years of college on the road. Kerouac had started the movement two decades earlier, but we still drifted in his wake. I was impelled by a notion that the full life must be rich in many varieties of experience—the farther from one's base point, the better. In the summer of 1973, my friend Donna and I headed east using our thumbs, following the Trans-Canada to Prince Edward Island and Nova Scotia, with side trips of camping in the Quebec bush, and dashing south to New York City in a bid to escape Maritime downpours. Donna found a good-looking boy with a dog; I found my own face staring back at me in the nighttime window of a Greyhound bus. My father's relative who lived in Queens had dispatched us home no sooner than we arrived on his doorstep. His journey had been an escape from war-torn Europe by leapfrogging to Antwerp and across the ocean to Cuba, where he was nursed through a bout of malaria by a young Romanian refugee who became his wife. He loved me, but he loved my hand-wringing father more. I'd spent six weeks on the road out east yet, among other things, missed the reversing falls outside St. John.

On finishing college, everyone planned to move out west, the Mecca of emerging lifestyles. Summer on the road seemed like a sensible dry run. My friend Stacey and I joined two boys to drive across the country. We'd met them through a radio ad: need a ride, share the gas.

The drivers were a disappointment. Sticking together in the back seat, Stacey and I could not have made those boys feel more inconsequential. As a result, they pounced upon the Trans-Canada, determined to shred it by sheer speed. So long Ottawa Valley, Algoma, amethyst mines of Lake Superior's north shore. Adios, Lake of the Woods. The third morning we awoke at the side of the highway and facing the wrong direction.

We ditched the boys at Lake Louise, intending to explore on our own by embracing nature. In the tenting grounds, the rangers clanged pots to chase away bears along with any atmospheric nocturnal rustlings. Because we were city gals, the bears a daunting deterrent, we followed the road instead of hiking up to Moraine Lake. Atop the Continental Divide, we snapped some pics before scrambling back before dark. The mountains were glorious, but a July squall blew us out. A bull-necked bald guy, who had a daughter resembling the pig-tailed murderess in *The Bad Seed*, gave us a ride to the Okanagan, promising "God's country so hot you can fry an egg on the pavement." Indeed, the Kelowna hostel offered only a paved lot for a campground. Next day, we couldn't hitch a ride from the famous cement floating bridge. We took a bus to Vancouver, laughing hysterically through the Okanagan Valley, and incredulous that the bus sign read Death's Head, which accounted for the driver's announcement of every patch of asphalt where a motorist or cyclist had given up the ghost.

I was just about to give up on travel as a transformative medium when Victoria burst upon us in almost phantasmagoric floral abundance. A shimmering light, reflected from the water in the harbour, festooned the downtown, and exalted the profusion of Anglophilic food and woollens' shops. During the eighteen months my family had spent in London, England, my sister had picked up an accent she refused to relinquish, though it posed a liability later in Montreal during the early years of the Quiet Revolution.

Knowing nothing of Victoria's nostalgia for things British, I wasn't prepared to be cast back, albeit to a glowing version. The England I remembered had been perpetually grey, dissolving in my sad little tears. I'd lost my big sister to school there. It's where I first felt alone. Suddenly, school as an ideal suggested itself in a storefront of uniforms. Not the lowly tunics and teddy blouses we'd worn in Montreal but kilts, plaids, box pleats, striped ties and scarves, and, most representative of all, the item worn by every schoolgirl every day of her London life, the classic indigo mackintosh. A visceral force sucked me to the glass. My sister had been an exceptional student. In England, she was put ahead a year despite her initial language handicap. In Montreal, she was bumped up again. She started McGill University at fifteen. When her name was put forward in referral for a scholarship to a US graduate school, my parents said, "What for? A girl is better off as a schoolteacher." The mackintosh was meant to be ours, and I was meant for the mackintosh. Stacey and I pooled our last dollars so I could buy it. The coat had seized me by the lapels, hauling me back to class.

At twenty-one, just finishing first-year university, I moved in with Craig. Yet another callow, gentile youth, my parents despaired. But worthy, oh, so worthy, I countered. Smart and fine, ethical, determined, deep. I saw an artist's sensibility grafted to his athletic rigour. It had been five years since my great love had dropped me. I had not fallen for anyone since except a string of safely unavailable professors. All those older men I had pined for, but it was a younger man I took as my mate, a man I felt reasonably sure I wouldn't lose myself to again.

Donna and Stacey made good on their mission to move west. Only one of them returned. Both became followers of the Unification Church. Donna was assigned a husband at a mass wedding officiated by the Reverend Sun Myung Moon in Madison Square Garden in 1982. By then I'd finished graduate school and was pregnant with our first child. Donna got pregnant upon marrying her stranger. Stacey had returned to Montreal in a box. She died selling flowers for the church, killed at dusk by a hit-and-run. Never married, yet her shroud was a wedding gown so—what? She wouldn't ultimately miss out? The macabre travesty of the wedding dress appalled me. But hadn't I, too, feared missing out? Didn't I suspect that deep down, below talent and intelligence, I was broken, not a fit companion for a specimen male of the species? Out of step with my politics and my times, the anachronistic anti-wisdom of my child mind had prevailed.

That I so narrowly missed falling into the hands of the Moonies wasn't lost on me. One is tempted, after the fact, to read confluences as portents: Donna's and my simultaneous pregnancies as a sign of forever friendship sundered by fate; the ride Stacey and I took to Death's Head as an omen of the sad waste of her life. Or to draw some connection between Mrs. Bruce's breakdown and the repeated crises of depressive anxiety and mania that tormented my late husband out of existence. Did I, beginning in childhood, feel an affinity for those made vulnerable by an unusual streak to their natures?

It seems ridiculous that an item of clothing in a strange city's shop window may have saved my life. It certainly changed the course of it by flagging my attention and halting my progress down a road that ultimately led my friends somewhere that for once I might have agreed with my parents was a dead end. The coat reminded me of their great gamble in leaving their country of origin when they were no longer young, so—in line with the simple trope of most immigrants—their children might have a better life than that country offered. Suddenly, I was aware not just of the promise my sister had embodied, the belt of the mackintosh cinched loosely around her uninflected juvenile waist, but also of their hopes for me however I had mocked these and deemed them superannuated. While Canada would remain terra incognita to my father—me and my friends a species alien to the world he had been raised in and mastered—I wasn't ultimately prepared to kick his faith in me in the teeth.

It took crossing the country, east and then west and back again, for me to change gears and switch tracks. While I knocked around aimlessly, the cachet of romance leached from the promise of travel much as romance had drained from love itself.

Strange Bedfellows

THE LAST I HEARD from Alex, one of the mistakes I made after my first boyfriend broke up with me, was through the entry intercom of the four-storey where Craig and I had our first apartment. I couldn't believe Alex had cajoled my mother into giving up my address. She had hated him on sight, pegging him right off as That Crazy One, and warning me that I would end up with a bullet through my brain like her sister Lili. The first time I heard this line, my mind came up short like a dog lunging from the end of a taut rope. Balked and baffled. Had she just implied that one of her sisters had died beforehand? A death unlike the ones I had taken in with mother's milk? A death deemed unsuitable for tender ears because it was committed as a crime of passion rather than by a process of systematic extermination?

My mother, who has now lost the art of verbal combat, once had a gift for getting in the last word. I'd had an answer to each of her objections. So what if Alex had a beard? That didn't make him a man; he was still just nineteen. And, yes, he was smart even if he wasn't in college. He read a lot and knew about music and had a steady job, so how could she say he was a reprobate just because he drove a motorcycle? But to argue with my mother was to play against a stacked deck. Having had enough of my claptrap, keening, she'd slapped down her trump.

"Hey," came the smoke-scored voice through the intercom. I recognized it immediately, and with it came an image of sitting with Alex on the cement slab in front of my parents' duplex. We each held a cigarette. I wanted to take his hand, but it would have mortified my mother in front of the neighbours. All the fervour was in my voice. "Any place, any time, you'll see. I'll always be there for you. Just find me." His little snickery sneer showed he knew best. "You'll see," I insisted. He took a long drag.

I held the receiver to the intercom away from my ear in case he picked up my pounding pulse. There were three flights of stairs between me and Alex, who would have legitimately qualified as a man by now. It made me sensitive to the fact that secretly I thought of Craig as a boy only recently graduated from the suburbs. He hung back to follow my lead, and not just around the city. How could he not now detect this disturbance in our field? His head bent over the page of his book as if it were my business alone to handle what came up.

"Hey, you," a smile in the familiar rasp. "Mission control, you up there?"

"Yup, me and my boyfriend."

"Yeah, your mom didn't sound so happy about him, either." The snicker.

It took me right back, as if I hadn't gone through a series of discarded selves since then: the dropout, the fuckup, the nut job whose gassed grandfather tromped around in her head—too skinny, too fat, a self-condemned social exile before I trusted my vision enough to picture a future. Alex dragged me back with a "Hey, you," so that a boyfriend didn't count, nor three years. He could walk through a door, and before I knew it, he'd have me on a mattress, his answer to everything. I had to remind myself I'd reached the age of majority, had a vote.

"I don't know what my mother told you. Things are different. I'm different. She doesn't like that we're living together, but she likes him. What do you want, Alex? Why are you here when you know I have a boyfriend and am back at school? My mother must have told you. How did you get her to give you my address?"

"Hah! Is it that hard to push the buzzer? Maybe you're not the only one who's changed."

"Whatever you want, leave me out of it, Alex. Leave my mother out of it."

The pitch brought me too close to getting drawn in, so I hung up the intercom. I checked the lock on the kitchen door to the fire escape. I pulled the drapes closed above the sink, intent not to slip on the oil slick that was Alex. I was too new, just like the thing with Craig. It's what Alex did. If you opened yourself just a crack, he poked holes in what you thought was solid and then oozed his way into them. The hollowness of my childish promise to him pointed an accusing finger, but I'd take shame over losing hard-won ground. In the living room, standing over Craig stretched out on the couch, I stated the obvious, "That was Alex Bailey. Crazy Alex."

"Well, he must have gone now," he said, erasing everything in my life before his time.

"Mummy! What were you thinking to give Alex Bailey my address?" I yelled into the phone, seeking to lay blame one way or another.

"So what?" she said. "He didn't sound that bad."

* * *

When one bandies around the epithet 'crazy,' just how often is the pot calling the kettle black? My mother's shrewd insights didn't owe much to analysis or logical corroboration, both of which she held in disdain. I'd walk into the house, and with one look, she'd unerringly demand who I had let make free with my physical charms. Despite my being a prudish early teen, she spotted something in my bearing that gave me away each rare time I tested even the most tepid of those waters. Alex had entered my mother's kitchen without the deference we children of the fifties paid our friends' parents—waiting to be spoken to, offering to clear the table, using Mr. and Mrs. frequently—polite ploys to distract them from our business. But Alex was the same with everyone. His springy, slightly bow-legged stride bore him straight into her domain. Hands digging in the pockets of his caked-looking jeans, he said, "Hi

Judy's mom," without waiting to be introduced, punctuating it with a kind of "hee-hee" that sliced through thin lips.

The perpetual five o'clock shadow and generally swarthy, pirate-like mien made him seem much older than the rest of us.

"*What* was *that*!" my mother charged after he left. "Are you out of your mind?"

A recurring question for me over the years was how to distinguish exceptionality in anyone—myself included—from illness. The long view shows I had willfully overlooked a sign about Alex that was more glaringly obvious than what had met my mother's eye. In the days of one-telephone households, the extension cord had been our lifeline to privacy. I could drag the phone into my bedroom, and if I happened to be in the bath, as I was when Alex first called me, it followed me there too. Briefly, before he left school mid-semester after repeating several years, he'd been in my grade-eleven North American literature class. I dismissed him as I did most classroom disrupters. Hearing his name after my mother, eyebrows raised, passed the phone into the bathroom was a puzzle. For the next two hours, I was swamped with examples of comments I had made on the songs of Bob Dylan, Joni Mitchell, and Gordon Lightfoot, that our oh-so-with-it teacher had added as leavening to the otherwise dated curriculum. She stood out among our teachers not only because of her avant-garde tastes and lesson plans. She carried her left hip behind her like the rump of a centaur, a disfigurement of birth or accident that because of her sympathetic sensibilities made her students tender towards her. Even Alex's backtalk in her class was less badgering and more like friendly teasing. He seemed to have total recall of each time I had raised my hand, annotating my remarks now with detailed references to the discography of our favourite folk singers, and illustrating their themes through his personal cast of larger-than-life characters: furious Floyd his father, his mom Glynis the weary, his brother Jimmy Dean, Jimmy Dean, why do you have to be so goddam mean, and finally his former best friend Walter the Crackpot.

Walter the Crackpot was why Alex kept a gun hidden in his tiny, partitioned half of an attic bedroom. I was to become a frequenter of this bedroom and familiar with the work of Walter firsthand. The house was a revelation in that I had never been in, nor known anyone to inhabit a hovel. Floyd wasn't furious so much as flaked out whenever we passed his whale of a corpus comatose on the living room couch, the mound of his hairy belly breaching both undershirt and unzipped pants. "F-ing asshole." Alex didn't bother to lower his voice as we circumnavigated the obstruction on our short route to the stairs. Floyd wasn't the only thing in the house that was too up close and in your face. Walter's mural in Alex's triangle of space under the eaves covered the wall, such as it was, above the mattress on the floor. As I stared up from under Alex's inveterate horniness, the hooves of the horses writhing in anguish on the wall hung just above my cranium. In time, I would recognize the painting by its original at the Museum of Modern Art in New York. It was supposed to be proof of Walter's brilliance and hand-in-glove excitability. Alex didn't say why Walter had turned on him. Nor did he add, or perhaps Walter had failed to mention, that Walter's mural was a copy of Guernica.

Somehow, I glossed over the fact of the gun. Hearing that word, did I try to hide my gasp as I had been hiding the fact that I lay naked, prune-fleshed, and motionless in the cold bath? I couldn't figure out what to do with that bizarre revelation. Certainly, I kept it to myself. It was after Alex came by a couple of weeks later, boldly presenting himself to my mother, that she dramatically unveiled her Ta-da! "A man like that! You could end up like your aunt Lili with a bullet through your head!" I gasped audibly at my mother's uncanny perspicacity, as though the trace of oiled gun metal had lifted off Alex, wafting through her red-and-white kitchen. Raising her nose, she had whiffed it.

The girls in my mother's family of seven children had been destined for Auschwitz, while the two boys, theoretically in less need of his protection, had been permitted by their father to leave Hungary before the war to establish themselves elsewhere. My sister and I had heard tales about them all, but when I thought now of my aunt Lili, I realized there was really nothing I could associate with her other than that she'd had a son and he, too, seemed hardly more than a name—Tibi. Lili, I had assumed, would have gone to the gas with her son; what else?

"Yes, no." Agitated, my mother waved off my questions, ignoring the fact that she herself had been first to kick the hive of the redacted past. "Tibi, of course, a child, he was gassed. But before that a rejected lover blew Lili's brains out, his own as well. Enough! It can happen. Don't think you know everything about everyone, like that man. What can a man like that want with a school girl? Nothing good, do you hear me?" she ranted. For emphasis, she switched from Hungarian to English, only slightly emending the phrase: "End of the story!"

Rejected lover? Lili had been married, right? Had a son, so she'd had to be. How could there have been suitors, thwarted or otherwise? My mother glared, prepared to swallow me whole.

My sister was already married. As such, my mother had taken to confiding in her woman to woman, unfazed by a daughter's squirming discomfort: "It's hard to pin Mummy down. On the one hand, it seems clear that Lili was murdered. They lived a high lifestyle until the tap got turned off. Something to do with politics after the Germans took Czechoslovakia. A Czech province transferred over to Hungary, and Lili's husband's fortunes rested on Czech government contracts which were voided. Something like that. Suddenly they were poor, and some old friend shows up from Palestine, and he mysteriously has lots of money and starts hanging around and basically bails them out. Lili complained that he was pressing her, but her husband didn't take notice, probably because of needing the guy's money. They were found locked in the bathroom, a bullet through her forehead, and the lover's face blown off. This is kind of weird though. She left a note bequeathing her jewellery to her sisters and saying she couldn't write anything more because she was too nervous. So was she part of a suicide pact rather than a victim of murder? Don't ever suggest that to Mummy or she'll flip. The papers dredged up every sordid possibility. The family was besieged by publicity on top of being bereft. So if you want to know why Mummy's so uptight about what people think about who you bring home, what time you come in, and if a motorcycle is parked in front of the door, maybe you won't try so hard to drive her crazy."

It was easier to keep Alex off-site once he had his apartment in the university ghetto where students had moved into cheap rentals vacated by waves of new immigrants. Alex's building was recent, a brown brick blight between weary Victorians. He could afford it because he was no longer at school. We'd press the button beside number 302, and some-one would buzz us in without asking who was there. Sometimes, if he was working a late shift at the Canadian National Railway yards where he'd picked up a job by grace of Floyd's seniority, Alex came to the door scratching his belly. Other times he'd be asleep. We entered, tossing our coats onto a heap on the floor of the open coat closet, just a few feet from the boot tray that spilled slush on to the parquet. Anyone could help themselves to peanut butter and bread on the kitchenette counter and browse through the stacks of LPs. There was never a moment without music.

After I quit school, too, I'd inevitably end up at Alex's apartment at some point in the day. Someone from the group would be there or show up eventually. The key was under the mat. Our coterie included three boys besides Alex, and a fluid flock of girls. The apartment cemented his centripetal hold on us. The glassy, fixed bead of his dark eyes demanded not only attention but also belief in his rhetoric. He was full of words, pronouncing upon anything—music, politics, ways of being existential or otherwise—an oracular spate that sucked up the air. Even so, we felt selected. He'd looked into our souls, discovering in them something real. We hungered for an authenticity that existed only outside our homes and communities. Authenticity resided in grunge, risk, a bare-knuckled grappling with the dark.

Some of the girls had sex with him, but with others like me, it was just making out. Even with those who were just friends, the potential for sex was omnipresent. Some feature might grab him, and his eye might fall where it hadn't before. That girl suddenly became the best thing, better than peanut butter and jam, not that he stuck to one diet, but she became the new dish against which all the others would be measured. For our own good, he let the rest of us know where we came up short. As with any pasha, the boys stayed clear of his harem. A girl interested in one of them maybe shouldn't have come around.

I was still fixated on the boy who had broken up with me more than a year before. I went to the apartment in the ever-present hope of bumping into him there or, failing that, into his better-looking best pal whom I hoped might convey a positive report of me. I would fall prey to Alex's lust when no one else was around as did the other girls who came upon him when he was alone. Once, I blundered onto someone equally startled by my arrival. Her distinctively wonky hip foiled her attempt to lurch up from the mattress on the living room floor. Did I stare or glare my shock? Could Alex leave no woman unutilized?

Barely two years after the Manson murders, there wasn't a parent in North America unaffected by the spectre of a cult that might turn their offspring into zombies. Looking back, I see how even a character as Manson-lite as Alex might have steered our dinghy out to sea had we not one by one abandoned ship. I was next to follow Walter's defection. Most of us had been drawn to a 'hard-to-herd' quality in each other. We were one-offs. A skillful sociopath might have worked this to his advantage, but Alex lacked a system. Nor was he evil. What he had was a knack for drawing people out of their spheres and into an atmosphere particularly conducive to his organism. Every so often, he turned against one of us. When this happened, the guilty party was accused of 'playing mind games' and 'fucking with his head' à la Walter the Crackpot whose crime remained sinisterly hazy. Alex was instinctual, acting on what he guessed rather than on what he deduced. In this, he was not unlike my mother. I never knew how I'd misstepped. We were all hanging out as usual in the apartment when he vice-gripped my arm, and with the other hand yanked open the frozen door to the balcony. He thrust me outside, locked the door, pulled the blinds shut, and left me coatless and bootless in the icy dark to examine my soul. No one dared to intervene, not even the boy who'd once said he loved me. Maybe it was because of him, because everybody knew that for me it was all about him, and if he hadn't dropped me, I'd never have taken up with Alex. I was supposed to feel culpable. I was supposed to cry uncle. Eventually, Alex left for work, and someone opened the balcony door. I grabbed my belongings. Better to feel my own way through the dark. Try as he would, and he did for a while, I didn't even nuzzle his bait.

* * *

What I resented was that my mother didn't trust me, trust in my resilience; that she, eternally dubious about anyone but herself, refused to apply her unerring sixth sense to my internal rudder. At the time, 'anorexia' was not yet a common term, nor was the word 'depression' used to refer to more than a mood. Perhaps I was lucky to have been left to flounder unlabelled. Not that my parents didn't worry. They pleaded with me. They shouted. They sent me here and there to be positively influenced. As much as I struggled, I was also free to find my own footing. On one count, I was certain. Whatever tempests raged through me, the pith would hold firm. How could she not tell? It seemed grossly undermining of my efforts to right myself. She who could sniff out whatever mattered most to her—whether I was sufficiently chaste and decorous in the eyes of near strangers—would not give me the benefit of her prevailing doubt.

For my mother, the worst that could befall a female loved one was what had happened to her sister, Lili. Incredibly, not the gas and the crematoria and the bombs that stole her other sisters and everyone else who had ever mattered to her. Lili's death stood out as the tragedy that had pierced my mother through when she still had the luxury of feeling a single loss acutely. She grieved the loss of Lili's life and the loss of Lili's love and the loss of Lili's precious reputation, the tally of which was a coherent world where something like a reputation still held water.

Was it not then a gift to find herself once more in circumstances where she might protect a loved one's reputation and fear for her singular life? I shouldn't have begrudged her. Each time she pulled out the threat that beat inside her like a living heart—I had better watch out or I'd end up like her sister Lili with a bullet through my head—she called up a world that could still make sense.

I think I might have seen Alex's gun once. He never took it out or held it in his hand. I never touched it. When I remember the gun, I see him pulling back either his pillow or the over-worked mattress on the floor of the attic bedroom. Maybe he opened a drawer to give me a flash. Only he and my mother actually saw it.

Found and Lost

I EXPECTED MY MOTHER TO launch into an excited account of her new grandchild before I even took off my coat. My sister's second baby had come into the world just before I was due home for Christmas break. Instead, my mother surprised me by surging into a report of my former best friend Cerise, whom she'd run into while buying groceries in our neighbourhood Steinberg's. Cerise's presence in our Steinberg's as opposed to the one in the Beaugrand Shopping Centre closer to her parents' flat was somehow astonishing. Cerise had a baby, too, and now lived in a duplex just a few blocks away. As a rule, my mother undermined whomever I currently held in repute. She had considered my high school friends beneath me in ability and a social standing more applicable to pre-war Mitteleuropa. Cerise had dodged her contempt by dint of an asset that overrode all else.

"Not one bit changed. The same beauty. I told her you'd be home soon for the holidays and would love to drop in."

Evidently, Cerise Donahue still looked at twenty-three as she had at sixteen, like the young Elizabeth Taylor of National Velvet. It had never been clear to me why my mother relished my playing handmaid to Cerise's beauty. Looking back, I wonder if it was the next best thing to my paying respect to her. When my sister and I looked good, it reflected well on our mother, but I think she derived even greater satisfaction from the fact that, however nicely we fixed ourselves up, at our best, we still fell in her shadow. Our lukewarm reception of this innate superiority had proved a disappointment. Perhaps now that I was in graduate school and thought so highly of myself, a little renewed exposure to Cerise's lustre might help me see things in a clearer light. For girls, education was a material asset useful in attracting a professional man, or if marriage failed, as practical employment training. Too much of it was a profligacy of time and money. I suspected that my sister, who had a better head for book learning than I did, would have benefitted more from graduate school. Nonetheless, I was quite smug about being the only one in our family to make good on the opportunity, and I'm sure my mother found my high opinion of myself, rare as it was, galling. She basked in our successes mostly when they were on her terms. Perhaps this is why I anticipated the worst from her motives. But what if my mother, who had a cast of mind about sex that might have been at home in a nunnery, endorsed my friendship with Cerise and her notorious allure because she would draw off all the rakes of Dunton High School, leaving my mother's little virgin inviolate? Who, the voice of many years asks, are we to look the gift horse of love in the mouth, however mangled the form in which it is offered?

The baby who ricocheted around Cerise's upper duplex kitchen in his rolling walker was a year old. Cerise had answered the door in a pastel sweater set that could have been paired with a poodle-appliquéd A-line from the fifties. She served tea perched straight-backed on her kitchen chair, presuming a kind of queenly exemption from the times based on a sense of her exceptional looks. She mentioned that she still took ballet classes a couple of times a week. She had hated living in Edinburgh where her husband had been taking his graduate degree in English. He was our point in common, she nodded, grad-school, literature studies, Jewish. She stressed the last, given that the members of my family had been practically the only Jews in Montreal's east end. He had given up Edinburgh for her, she continued, transferred back to their alma mater, McGill, whereas I, it was left unsaid, had given her up. I took in what I imagined of her life in the suburban duplex, confined like her baby in his walker careening from wall to wall over the same ground. I thought of my classes, the readings I had to do for the seminars I'd lead, the undergraduate papers yet to be marked, and the stories I would write in lieu of a major paper. I thought of the famous author who was my advisor on the project. And I allowed myself to remark, "What do you do with all your time?"

* * *

Five years before this, I'd been about to crack the chrysalis of a self-imposed isolation that had spanned almost two years. My boyfriend had left me when we were in grade ten. In grade eleven, I quit school. I also left home for a while. What I'd said to Cerise in trying to explain why I hadn't wanted her in my life anymore was that being friends with her got in the way of my "feeling good about myself." Or perhaps being friends with her made me feel bad about myself.

Cerise Donahue and I had been best friends from the first year of high school. Both of us dancers, although she was classically trained, almost a pro. I would attend her classes like watching a performance. We danced together in her bedroom in a duplex upper unit on St. Donat, south of Sherbrooke Street, not in the new suburb north of Sherbrooke where, my mother would have pointed out, we owned a whole half. Cerise and I danced in the three feet between her big bed and her vanity console and, on the other side, in the narrow space between the bed and the stereo cabinet that once must have been purchased for the living room. Cerise was the prized member of her family because of her looks and her brains, in that order. If she'd called dibs on the master bedroom, she'd probably have been handed that too. We gave ourselves over to the Supremes, Neil Diamond, Carole King, and the Stones, in the constricted margins between the bed and the walls. When we finally tumbled exhausted from dancing and talking cross-legged on the bed about her boyfriends and books and the pros and cons of each other's bodies, we slept spooned up, her thick hair warming the back of my neck. Four years is a long time in a young life that measures a year by the various attitudes, credos, and friends she has tried on like outfits. Cerise and I survived my incarnations save the last one that stopped staring into windows as though they were mirrors. The one that wiped off her lip gloss and eyeliner and chose loose blouses with rough embroidery my mother said only a peasant would be caught dead in. The word 'peasant' in my mother's mouth meant anti-Semite and to be despised.

Donna Moreno was a step in a new direction as I prepared to resume social contact. She wasn't like Cerise, who hogged the spotlight; or the boy who had dropped me because he couldn't get it up when we tried to go all the way; or the next one, more a man than a boy, who threw me out into the cold. Donna and her little sister kept house for their dad in a two-bedroom apartment in a white brick low-rise on Hochelaga East. A Tabagie, a Mac's Milk, a barber shop, and a dry cleaner's shop occupied the building at street level. Just a few steps took me from the Hochelaga bus stop on the corner to the steel-framed glass door wedged between the Mac's and the cleaners. Its dry chemical heat accosted the cold air that pushed in with me, herding me up the stairwell to the third storey. I made it to the apartment door, gasping. Her dad was out on the weekends. A rectangular, white, plastic laundry basket sat on the floor in the kitchen like a piece of furniture. Donna said they'd been here a few years since her mom had skipped out. I hadn't asked if they used to live in a house. Donna wasn't self-conscious about the apartment. She accepted me, too, such a gift, as it was more than I had managed.

I didn't call Donna my best friend right away. She was still best friends with Mila Vechinsky. For a while, the three of us hung out in greasy spoons, nursing mugs of percolated coffee in green bakelite cups. But once Donna and I spent more time together, we dreamed of a summer road trip led by our thumbs. I had finished high school at night school, and had taken my first year of college, forcing down my bitter boredom. I was way ahead of Mila when it came to giving up being a dutiful immigrant daughter. Whenever my parents mentioned university, I threatened to quit school again. I believed I 'thought for myself' and insisted on my right to act autonomously.

If one has wandered in a wilderness, it's safe to say one was once lost. Donna Moreno found me. I was a pebble she picked up and dusted off. It was a huge relief to see my best sides reflected back as though they sparkled. I had kept so much to myself for these two years, I was surprised to have a voice. Mila Vechinsky was tall, imposing, but chary with words. They spilled out of me like grain from an over-stuffed gunny sack, while Donna and I, jacked on caffeine, gabbed through the night. I was tired of hating school, of defying my parents, of letting myself down. Donna had heard of an alternative college program that stressed self-directed learning. We could apply. Really? And we should take an apartment together. I thought of having my own place, fantasized about never doing anything but sewing curtains. When I confessed, Donna laughed, "That'll be the day."

Donna Moreno and I decided to get in some training for the open road. The long weekend in May was warm enough to tent, we hoped, although Ottawa was further north than Montreal. It had turned mild enough to catch a ride in the open bed of a pickup. This was before seat belt laws. We could have starred in a Coke ad, two girls in overalls, hair streaking across our faces as we tore down the highway under a clear sky, the epitome of the new girl, the new age. Wind smacked. Our hair whipped, snarled, filled our mouths when we gasped, pitching over potholes.

We arrived in Ottawa late in the afternoon, the sky by this point lowering. No sooner did I jump down with another jolt to my innards than a groundswell in my abdomen heralded a familiar seepage. "Uh-oh," I said, "I think my period's early." Within a few blocks, I was no longer just seeping. We'd harboured a dream of a provincial park or a charming property outside the city where we might camp for a couple of nights. But the highway had flowed under us, bearing us relentlessly forward. Now that we were here, I needed a washroom and caffeine. We dropped our backpacks next to our chairs at the nearest diner. Within a half hour, I bled through two pairs of tampons. We found a pharmacy. I bought tampons and something I hadn't used in years, sanitary napkins, the thickest available, and then asked to use the washroom.

A few weeks earlier, I'd taken myself to the college clinic to be fitted for an IUD. I'd managed to seduce the boy who had dumped me. Hope springs stupidly. As the little crab was inserted, I levitated a foot off the examining table. The clinician said the following few periods might be heavier than usual. I was not as a norm a heavy bleeder. So it shouldn't be an issue, she'd assured me. Gingerly, feeling my insides might spill out with each footfall, I had headed towards the Metro and home. There, as I grovelled towards bed, I heard my mother call out from the kitchen that she'd warned me there was a flu going around, but did I ever listen?

Neither Donna nor I were alarmed. She stood outside one stall after another, in diners, gas stations, eventually on the university campus on the edge of town where we took shelter in the basement labyrinth, grateful for the facilities that were cleaner than usual since the summer semester hadn't yet started. We stowed our packs out of sight. When we heard the cleaning staff or the steps of a security guard, we hid in the toilet stalls from which we were never far. We dined on vending machine fare, not that I felt hungry. I craved coffee, tea, and chicken soup. The salty soup really hit the spot. I had never bled like this. Donna handed me wet paper towels beneath the doors. Then dry ones to line my underwear. I'd succeeded in stuffing four tampons in at once, carefully, with pads and paper towels to sop up the overflow.

The question of hemorrhage didn't occur to me even once. In my medical opinion, all that jostling on the highway had so shaken up the little crab, it wanted to claw its way out of my uterus. I actually felt lucky. Not once had my friend mentioned our messed-up weekend. Donna stood behind stall doors receiving the warm bundles I passed out to her. She hadn't drawn up her nose in a way that hid the divot in the middle that would let me know her anywhere, anytime, even when we would meet forty years down the road. She would step out of a car dressed unrecognizably in a sky-blue dress of some cheap synthetic material, a string of ugly brown glass beads bobbing against her bosom right down to her prominent midriff. She had turned into a matron from a provincial American town, the snob in me noted. Gone were the jeans and t-shirts and lumberjack plaids she had looked so pert in as a girl. Her long, straight hair used to hang in two sheets separated by a middle part. The t-shirts not-quite tight over her small, perfectly circular breasts with their incised nipples. The curvy rear flaring below a small waist. She'd been cute. Her nose was cute, too, more so because of the nick of flesh chipped out of it. I recognized her instantly by the divot and also by her smile, which was exactly the same, open as a child's but with a rueful tug at the corner. Despite the dress, the weight, the accruement of years, even had I not been waiting at our point of assignation, had we bumped into each other in a foreign landscape, I would have known her. It raised the question: once you're close to someone in your youth—and I was thinking of the kind of intimacy one rarely encountered again, less charged perhaps but no less deeply felt than romantic love—would you always feel connected? Was there a core self under the changes wrought electively or by the acts of time that one reached out to as a reflex?

Once, when we were both still undergraduates but at different universities, I met Cerise accidentally on the Sherbrooke Street bus. At this time, Donna and I were no longer best friends. I think she might already have moved to the West Coast. Or maybe she was on her international trek to Afghanistan. Relationships were fluid. We'd rushed in and out of each other's lives. Donna and I had travelled together, lived together, and, when she took an apartment with a boyfriend, I moved in with Stacey. Stacey would leave me high and dry to pay the rent by myself in the first term of my first undergrad year, so I'd have to break the lease and move into my married sister's dining room. Stacey moved next door to Donna and took up with Donna's boyfriend's best friend. Perhaps it was in my second year that I met up with Cerise, after they'd all moved out west. I barely heard from them anymore. I had chosen to continue my studies while they hit the road in that clichéd quest for self, a kind of quasi-spiritual seeking one's fortune.

Cerise jumped from her seat to hug me. For some minutes, as we raced to catch up on each other, my heart swelled. You love someone for years, and then you decide not to love them anymore, and perhaps you don't—perhaps that love withers without exposure to the light that was the time you spent in each other's company. But what if that love doesn't altogether die? There are plants in the desert that lie dormant for years and then burst into leaf at the first rare rainfall. I felt hope for that possibility. It felt so good to see her in her wool beret, hear her voice, and soak up her reciprocal pleasure. She was telling me about the boy she was in love with. With Cerise, there had always been a boy, but this one she actually loved. "He reminds me of you," she laughed, "smart, into books, and Jewish too. You could be related. He isn't tall either, but he has a broad back like yours." A broad back. I hadn't any idea what my face might have done. Many of my features were far from small. My arms, breasts, thighs were full. But I wasn't built large, and my shoulders and back were narrow. This Cerise well knew. We'd taken measuring tapes to each other's bodies and compared the data. We'd borrowed each other's clothes, knew where they'd fit tight or hang loose. Perhaps she couldn't help herself, didn't realize what she was doing, or had always done, jabbing me in the ribs, rapping me on the funny bone with her reminders that pretty is as pretty does, but beauty claims a field of its own.

* * *

It always pained me that Stacey proved merely a sidebar to my friendship with Donna. Donna and I drifted apart because she had a boyfriend she wanted to live with, and because in the lingo of the day, the gravitational pull of the academy was straightening me out, while Donna hit an increasingly spiralling path, eventually camping for months on Long Beach on Vancouver Island, and wandering from Morocco to Asia. Stacey moved into the spot that Donna had vacated, but the friendship between us didn't take. Something in Stacey was too eager to please and to follow. People took advantage of it. Sometimes it was tempting for me too. It didn't altogether surprise me that in October of my first term, she said she'd be moving out. Disrupted and irate, I still applauded her action. We were all in flux. It was time to do-si-do and switch partners.

Stacey moved next door to Donna. I didn't think much about her after that.

* * *

Returning to my parents' house after visiting Cerise and her baby, I was indignant with my mother for setting up the visit. She was fully aware that Cerise got under my skin. Ready to light into her, a shock went through me as she swept me up in her embrace. "*Yahy, yahy,*" she moaned in Hungarian, "your teacher from college called with very bad news."

By college, she meant the alternative program that Donna and I had attended during the year we'd shared an apartment. I kept in touch with this teacher, and had let her know I was in town.

"It's a tragedy," my mother said, releasing me. "That little girl, the one you had no time for, you know, the one from a good Jewish home, they had the funeral for her today."

For weeks after I took the train back to grad school, I pictured Stacey's face. Stacey as she was when she first arrived at college wearing the monochromatic ensembles her mother had picked out for her. Stacey with her thick, chestnut hair pulled off her forehead in a high ponytail tied by a scarf. Stacey, before she started dressing in patchouli-scented paisley. An oval, guileless countenance poised for approval. I had met her first. If not for me, she wouldn't have necessarily taken up with Donna or Donna's boyfriend's best friend. She wouldn't have followed them out west, right down to California where one of them was first recruited by the Moonies. In a domino effect, they toppled one after another into what at the time was perceived to be a cult.

The college grapevine filled with rumours about the religious sect none of us had heard of. Sleep deprivation, repetitive chanting and prayer, poor nutrition, all contributed to a kind of brainwashing that made the members biddable.

While marking papers, attending seminars, trying to stay focused on a new story, I dwelled on Stacey, the lamb led to slaughter. Our former teacher said she'd never seen anyone as stoved-in by grief as Stacey's parents and sister at the funeral of their beloved girl. I imagined their horror when they opened the casket of their dead child to find her tricked out as a bride. Of whom—Sun Myung Moon? Christ?

We had once thrown the *I Ching* together. We'd looked up the passage corresponding to her throw to see what her future held. "What the heck does that mean?" Her blameless brow had furrowed. "Who knows? It's just crap," I replied. But the passage was evident. It indicated no future in her forecast. I kept replaying that moment. By interpreting the passage to myself, had I sealed her fate?

During this period, I received a letter postmarked California. It was stuck all over with heart-shaped stickers, my name and address on the front printed in large, neat letters, the letter *i* in lower case, with a circle for the dot. Inside was a page of lined stationary, and if I hadn't flipped it over to read the signature I would have thought the letter was from a child of eleven or twelve. The cursive was large and loopy, adhering to the lines with deliberate care, the i's all dotted in cute little circles. Hand-drawn hearts and daisies floated in the margin. This was the first I'd heard from Donna in at least three years. She made no mention of our dead friend. The tone was literally hearts and flowers. I found no trace in it of the person I had loved, who had kidded around when I passed my bloodied napkins under the door of countless bathroom stalls. Who, when I awoke flooded with panic after smoking too much dope at a college farmhouse retreat, locked us into the bathroom where I might sleep in the tub with the light on, while she stretched out on the bath mat like a trusty dog. She'd parented her sister more consistently than either of their parents had. The voice of the letter was vapid and insipid for a woman in her twenties. I didn't have to be told that something strange had befallen my old friend.

There was a crux, the last moment our lifelines had intersected. We had just finished college but didn't know what to do next. We had heard a lot of talk about going out west where everything (whatever that meant) was happening (another ambiguous term). We were lounging about the college common room, although the semester had concluded, when our forthright teacher took one look at us, perched her fists on her hips, and declared in disgust, "You people make me sick. Don't you have anything useful to do with yourselves? You!" she singled me out with the authority of a prophet. "Put yourself out of your misery and register at university this minute!" I had written stories for this teacher's workshop. I had attended her women's studies seminar. A credible signpost was pointing me in a direction that, however mainstream and uninspired, made sense. It hadn't been easy trying to straddle two horses. Plunking down onto one saddle, I headed west along Sherbrooke to the Loyola campus. Donna and Stacey bolted off on the other.

The letter's infantile drivel sickened me. I ached with the loss of one friend dead, and another mentally despoiled. I was certain she was wrong in the path she had taken. It had led her to the well down which she had dropped, dragging the tractable Stacey with her. I wanted to hit her hard, knock out the damaging dogma that had displaced her ineffable sweet and sensible self. I wrote back saying it was her fault Stacey was dead.

* * *

Anyone who's had a child knows that from the minute that child is born to the day she goes to kindergarten, one is hard pressed to find a free moment, let alone not know how to pass the time. At some point, my mother told me that Cerise had moved to Toronto where I was by then living. Even my parents had moved. After living among gentiles for over two decades, they bought a condo in a west-end Jewish enclave, reverting instinctively to running with their pack. As fate would have it, she met Cerise at the local upscale mall and raved to me afterwards about Cerise's two kids, especially the little girl, her spitting image, already at five, you guessed it.

Cerise was in Montreal visiting her mother, the Irish expat now living near Cerise's Jewish in-laws. I had married the boy I'd moved in with during my second year at Loyola. Then came grad school for me and, later, teacher's college for him. At his job interview in a small city in northern Alberta, the principal strongly suggested we should be married if Craig hoped to be given the position. By then I figured we'd start a family anyway, so no biggie.

No biggie. What would my sister have said had she known how disdainful I'd been of her for giving up graduate school on our parents' say-so, then marrying and having children? Probably she had. Some eyes took longer than others to adjust to the dark, but my career path would remain unlit. I'd remain at a loss as to why I hadn't liked teaching or working in the world. I wished, though, that it had felt less like capitulation to have pursued what kept me at home: a psychologically fragile husband who bore much watching over, writing, raising kids, and occasionally sewing curtains.

After I'd had my first baby, I tried to look Cerise up in Toronto under her maiden name. My milk brain at the time had permanently erased her husband's surname. I didn't find her in the telephone listings nor on the internet or Facebook in the coming years. I'm not even sure I would have brought up the remark dropped when I was unduly certain of myself, before I put down my pen for years to become a full-time, home-based wife and mother. I did write one book once my youngest was out of diapers, but I should add that my sister wrote eight. Recently, I learned that Donna Booth née Moreno wrote one too. Self-help, no less.

Donna proved more proficient on the internet, finding me—again. She had business in Toronto. I rifled through my closet for a patchwork vest that might call up our past. Despite her unforeseeable outfit, I knew her immediately. She still belonged to the Unification Church. Over lunch, she kept asking if I didn't feel a need for a more spiritual life. Repeatedly, I pressed her on questions about chanting and brainwashing and tithes. Neither of us seemed ready to accept at face value the answers we were given. We picked up something else, the timbres of our youthful voices and the place, the emotional terrain we had traversed together. We leaned into that patch, recognizing what? The essential natures most apparent in youth before life has tested and reshaped us; our young selves preserved in amber? It would have been nice to be able to let a little rain fall on that spot reserved all these years for the other.

In Sickness and in Health

LOVE IS JUST LOVE, as much as we'd like to believe in its magic. My love for Craig had the legs of an arranged marriage, yet I had nothing but faith in its magical properties. He wasn't the man my parents would have chosen—a vector primed for success. Not this unfledged youth who had repudiated his family and had little yet to show for himself. I arranged the match of my own doing, listing his attributes and strengths as if to convince a younger, more headstrong, romantic self. This did not prove me any less rash than had I tumbled into mind-swiped passion. I believed I'd make it work, understanding ahead of those who start out in love before running aground on the shoals of proximity, that it would take application. I was a fervent believer. In myself, foremost, the restorative power of my positive affections. And in the man Craig would as a result not transmute into but revert back to, the person he was born to be—as if such a one exists—before the wrong kind of love had marred him. But love is just love. We feel it. We give it. It doesn't undo the past. It isn't an agent of epigenetic reversal such as we've dreamed of picking up at the pharmacy in some fortunate future. In 1975, we hadn't coined the term, let alone the notion of environmental factors that might effectively switch on latent expressions in our genes. Hope rises eternal, often to be debunked. In the seventies, we still trusted in the theories of psychoanalysis. I believed we could change ourselves through love and self-scrutiny. Perhaps it's too harsh to say my marriage became the laboratory. Perhaps I tax my youth too heavily. What about good intentions, steadfastness? Two children raised in health and accomplishment? What about love?

My story, like most everyone's, starts with my parents. When I first tried writing about them, Craig reacted swiftly. Why them? What made me think anyone would be interested in the experiences of two unremarkable people? An intelligent man in his mid-twenties, old enough to have known better. Many years later, fighting to regain his life after debilitating mental illness, he indirectly became their stories' chief promulgator by serving as my literary agent. I think he'd say the same thing now about being turned into a subject. He'd hate it. I see the long, sharply squared-off face, the eyes permanently turned down from too often pleading against his pain. I hear his bitter dismissal of the stupid idea: why would I think anyone would be interested in such a sorry case?

We have but one life, although it's not the only one we might have had. My parents' histories shaped mine. Who am I but for those historic circumstances, and how might I discharge that debt? Was there ever any question but that I'd find my way to Craig? Perhaps what he'd hate is what he always knew. He would never be fully the subject any more than I had fully belonged to him. Why is love not sufficient? Why should there be oneness? In truth, we weren't separate enough. When Craig's jaw yawned open to the psychotropic drugs that dragged on the muscles holding up his long torso, shame suffused the cells in my skin as though I myself had folded over in defeat: I reflected in him, and he reflected in me, neither of us singly whole.

If I am who I am, become nothing more in the eyes of the world than when I started, an outcome of stasis poised on the head of a pin, no more apt to fall than to fly, it is because of two unremarkable people's remarkable losses. I define myself by my father's murdered family, foremost his six-year-old daughter whose unlived destiny I've left unfulfilled. On my mother's side pile the bodies of her loved ones, all of whom she refused to memorialize ritually, heaped as they were among the mounds of naked limbs and trunks unyielding in the doneness of their anonymous deaths. "Agency," I'm reminded by my Canadian friends, is a state of mind and to be cultivated. But what sway personal agency against this overwhelming refutation? I have balanced all my life between belief in the power to create oneself anew and a sense of futility.

Craig, on the other hand, resolved to be self-made. He ran away from home at age seventeen. We don't know what propelled him. He never said, because he didn't himself know or he would not divulge. During our twenty-five years together, he stuck to his story about taking off just like that and refusing further contact. He said he didn't know why at that moment or what may have prompted him. He grabbed his father's duffel bag with all his father's paraphernalia as a referee still in it and threw a few of his own belongings on top of them. The arbitral underpinning at the base of Craig's identity? He had an unerring sense of fairness and for what was right. What might he have seen? What might he have done to make the flight from the sylvan suburbs into the city's affordable squalor his only recourse? I can never turn Craig inside out to reveal what lay within, only state what I observed and what he told me. In this way, I'm forced to honour his memory. I, on the other hand, expose my innards. Within lies a semblance of story. How do I cobble together Craig's?

* * *

I met the seventeen-year-old, soon-to-be-runaway at an alternative college program in its first year of operation. The school was small and experimental, along the principles of humanistic education. It attracted alternative types among both students and faculty. One could expect something either 'off' or counter-culturist about those in attendance. By all appearances, Craig belonged to the former category, I the latter, but if one looked below the surface, one would have found elements of both in each student. We were lucky that an alternative program happened to be offered just when we needed it. Judging by what he described of his background in sports, which would have had nothing in common with the program's aims of self-directed, interdisciplinary, wholistic learning, it was safe to assume that Craig was there for a refit. His parents had urged him to go to the national military academy. The words 'Royal' and 'Military' drew a collective gasp during an assembly at the start of the year. It was 1973, and the average length of hair among the boys sitting on the mosaic floor of the manor house that had formerly lodged an order of monks was well below the shoulder. The whole school community drew around the lost sheep to bring him into the fold.

We recognized one another through a story he wrote called "And You Want to Be the Best." Sports culture was outside my ken, but the suburbs weren't. When you're young, enamoured of your specialness, who doesn't hope for a crown? For Craig, not being best was to fail; there was no in-between. Coming second was always as degrading as kissing your sister, a legacy he'd never shake even after he'd traded his cleats for notebooks, novels, manuscripts, and, later, textbooks. He was driven and inspired by competition. Before we had children, I answered to the call of literature and personal inquiry. His writing may not have been the best, not even better than mine, but it showed talent, and, as we used to say then without cynicism, it rang true.

* * *

In the telling of our life together, upon what, amid the myriad of shared events and memories elbowing each other out of the frame, does one decide to focus? Which of the minutiae that filled our moments for twenty-five years feels realer than the rest? No, truer than the rest. Was not each lived moment real and true? All this sifting through the sands of our small life leaves me holding nothing. When Craig was suffering towards the end of his illness, our two sons leaned on me and cleaved to me as I to them. They've grown into their own lives. Now when I try to grasp something of those twenty-five years, it's as though our marriage had spread with Craig's ashes in the raw interior sea where we cast him. Diffused, ever more distant. Does one just grab, then, the random flotsam and jetsam that surface within reach?

Picture the seven-member Chambers family squeezed into a near-wreck of a car, driving the minimally ten-hour trip between Montreal and the farm on the Bruce Peninsula where Craig's mother had been raised. The car wouldn't have had air conditioning. How many times would they have had to stop to peel themselves from the vinyl seats when one of them had to pee? Did the kids shout for joy when the interminable stop-and-start ended? Did they pile out of the steaming sedan in desperate relief? I imagine even the youngest took one look at his Grandmother Chisolm's visage and buttoned it. The girls cast furtive glances from the barn to their grandfather's wryly welcoming grin and shrank back into the sticky seat. Even their mom Frances patted her hair self-consciously while picturing the flaws in her appearance, before swinging her peddle-pusher clad legs onto the dirt drive. Only Geoffrey bounded out, extending his hand in perennial good faith to his father-in-law's habitual rebuff.

"Grandfather," Craig, being the eldest, stuck his neck out as usual, "can we go to the beach before dinner?" It is all the children have thought about during the long drive. Seven miles of raked brown sand that tapered so gradually into deep waters, every one of them, however little, could splash, paddle, and jump in the waves in blessed release.

As small as a life is, and as short as Craig's was, there's no nutshell version. He came fully formed into my world as an adolescent boy bent on remaking himself, but his stories were elegies to the friends he'd left behind and to the great love who was his mother. Whatever she'd done, however warped her affection, it was real nonetheless and his big heart, his vast capacity for empathy must have owed something to it. He banished his family from his life for six years, until I wore down his resistance to meet with them again. We returned to Montreal from graduate school for the Christmas break, staying with my parents as usual. On that long held-off day, we caught the commuter train from Bonaventure Station, and his father, the man Craig had described as emotionally remote, inaccessible, picked us up at their stop. As much as Craig might have protected his mother from knowledge of herself, so he spurned his father, perhaps for doing nothing, for pretending nothing was amiss. But the man who came towards us in an unseasonal downpour, unmindful of the rain that drenched him as soon as he leapt from the car, a man so obviously dissolving as he took his tall, bony boy into his embrace, was not the man I recognized from Craig's accounts. He exuded warmth and affability, and as we sat in the living room of their mid-century bungalow, it was Frances who spoke in terse, truncated sentences, her smile, when she thought to, delayed as though she had to read it its lines. There must have been love in that family, or none of the five children could have grown up to raise children of their own, as they did, by all appearances having plenty to offer. *However.* One of the five, the firstborn and nearest to his mother's heart because he'd arrived after a series of failed pregnancies and before she succumbed to what motherhood would bring out in her, had run off with no intention of going back. Around the dinner table, the four other siblings, the girls especially in their odd cotton, almost Mennonite-style dresses, looked up shyly but knowingly from their plates, to snatch glimpses of their lost brother and his improbable girlfriend.

* * *

Craig and I had moved in together during the second year of my undergraduate program in Montreal. A honeymoon year one might have expected. We were both in psychotherapy. Somehow Craig must have gotten himself to his therapist in the months he was confined to bed with mononucleosis, strep, and the deciding punch that kept him there. I was at school most days. We each saw our doctors once a week. I remember mine nodding his head while regarding me with tolerance when I declared the topic of Craig off-limits. Muddying the waters, I called it. I didn't want anyone else's two cents muddying the waters of my seeing for myself how or if our relationship would work out. The only time he showed exasperation was when after three years I declared I'd been accepted into graduate school in another city and so would have to end the therapy. Did he think I was ready to terminate? What did it matter what he thought, he said a little testily, as I had already made up my mind without him? I'd considered the decision to move away from Montreal was a sign in itself of readiness. For what? To act alone? Separate from the proxy parental prop? Individuate? A testament to his self-management, he didn't explode. How could my therapy possibly be finished when we hadn't even begun to explore my mulish commitment to a depressed boy for whom I had yet to feel a sexual spark! These words he kept to himself, though they must have filled his mouth close to choking.

At graduate school, we lived in a toy-sized flat not ten minutes from the university, a luxury after commuting all my life around a big city. All we had to do was walk down our street, beneath the roar and rumble of the international bridge, and we were on campus. Craig had lost a school year to the mono, so he had yet to finish his undergraduate degree, while I was on a free ticket, the first time I could study without having to work part-time as well. No gas station or stockroom clerking, no waitressing or emptying bedpans in a nursing home. The gained hours felt like a windfall. Lest I developed too high a sense of my significance, the rundown flat set me right. A friend had come down for a weekend from Toronto to help me scour years of grease from the kitchen walls. She had to have been a good friend indeed to offer to clean the scummy bathroom Craig and I would share with the resident of the neighbouring flat, an arrangement I'd never come to terms with during our two-year tenancy. We steam cleaned the mossy carpet three times to get rid of its musk. The flat had come furnished, a mixed blessing requiring scrub, bleach, and polish to make our own; although the elbow grease of true friendship rather than that of both occupants turned it around. The landlords were a married couple, but we knew the woman better since she dropped by monthly to collect the rent from each of the four tenants of the subdivided house. She couldn't get over how we'd transformed the dive with art prints and throws. "Real cute," she'd say. "My stuff looks real cute in here," all her doing. Next door and upstairs, the faces kept changing.

Craig ate without protest anything I served up, however frugal and, to put it mildly, innovative. One evening as we raised our forks over a funky stew of chicken livers, the front door shut, and heavy, purposeful steps strode through the living room. She materialized within moments, tall, big-boned, a face that looked ploughed. The landlady, bearing a square handbag on her crooked arm in a parody of gentility. She cast a proprietary gaze over the scene, amused to have caught us off guard, launching without salutation into a warning against giving out her number, "like you been doing," to people inquiring about the flat next door if they were, "you know, them." She didn't say Black, but instead "not us, nice kids like you." I remembered the man who had knocked on our door that week to inquire about the rental.

Craig's chair scraped the floor. "That's illegal," he said. At six feet, he didn't stand much taller than the landlord.

"This is my house. I guess I can do what I want with it," she claimed.

"Not if you discriminate, which is against the law."

Clean walls were quickly forgotten, along with vacuumed carpets and waxed woodwork and rent received promptly in cash.

"I can throw you out on the street, you know. You and your smelly slop. You think you're special, but you're just dirty renters like the rest."

Craig didn't touch her. A sheep dog snapping at her borders, he nudged her doorwards. "Out," he said, "out of our home. Don't you dare disturb our supper."

I might have laughed under different circumstances. "People like that," I tried to the find words. "People like that—that. She could have been any of the ones who killed my parent's families." Craig had kicked the viper out, while I sat paralyzed. It gave me hope for our future.

"Supper," I said, finally giving way to hilarity. "Craig, imagine if we called the police to lodge a complaint about disturbing our supper."

We did have to call one day when scuffling and raised voices, the thud of something falling, came from the flat next door. Through the window we saw both landlords, husband and wife, tussling with the tenant in the doorway of his apartment. "Liar! Thief!" He was a recent arrival I barely recognized, slumped between his accusers, perhaps under the influence or under the weather. At any rate, he was no match for them. Craig rushed outside.

"You better let him go. You can't remove him by force. I told you. It's against the law."

"Go yourself, you stupid boy. You get out of our way. This here thief didn't pay up. You want to catch it too?"

I pulled at Craig's arm. He was buzzing, literally vibrating as he shook me off. "Go in, Judy," he pointed at our door. "Now. Call 911 right now!"

"Stupid. I'll show you, Stupid," the woman, more feral of the two, screamed. But she let go of the drooping carcass who came to life with alacrity and bolted inside.

Thereafter, we kept the Axis powers at bay by sending the rent by mail well before it was due at the end of each month. But I remained in the grip of a tableau I couldn't shake: Craig trembling as he faced the three-headed monster. I'd stood behind him, his waist-length hair a shield in which each unerringly straight strand arrowed down his back. Long, well-formed fingers had curled unnaturally into clubs issuing from the barrels of his ever-present flannel shirt. Voluminous bell-bottomed jeans with their trodden hems caught wind of the rage in his knees.

He was so affronted, through and through, that his hair, his shirt, his jeans, all so nearly known to me, had fused into a standard of war. Not a single atom in him had hesitated. It wasn't fear that shook him uncontrollably. That was the puzzle. The way the ultrasensitive Craig hurled himself into the fray without a thought. Shaking while molten lava poured off his slopes. Who was this?

After living with Craig for a quarter of a century, and hearing him tell me, some days for hours on end, what he was feeling, I cannot say I know what it was to have been Craig, or how he withstood an almost relentless form of suffering. Cycles of ups and downs that we came to identify as latently bipolar were proven by hindsight to have been there from the start, from before I ever met him. The boy on the ride mower in the cemetery, fired from his first summer job for being stoned. "I never even tried the stuff," he told me. Had the presence of death made him dissociate? For Craig, death was never a hypothetical shoved to a back burner of the mind. Hobbling through our first apartment on a phantom cane, his birthday an anathema. Eighteen-year-old crock, geezer, one decrepit step closer to oblivion. Latently bipolar, his doctors later claimed, although Craig was never really 'up.' 'High' for him was even keel for most. We continued lurching from a kind of strength to strength despite the recurrent crashes, for hadn't Craig always floundered and then rebounded? His wretched anxiety had not succeeded in holding him down. I had watched him haul himself back up, over and over, onto legs that as a boy had fully given out on him.

"How so?" I'd asked after we'd watched Antonioni's *The Red Desert* in which—during his parents' nasty divorce—their young son had pretended to lose the power in his limbs.

"Just like me," Craig said afterwards.

"What? You pretended to be paralyzed?"

"No, I was. Woke up one day without feeling in my legs."

"Really? Hysterical paralysis?"

"If that's what you want to call it."

"Not what I want, what you're saying happened. How come?"

A shrug. He had no intention of prodding that beast with a stick. I knew quite a bit about Craig and guessed more. Guess is the operative term.

* * *

Finishing graduate school for me was like stepping off the flat edge of the known world. I could no more envisage life beyond it than I could imagine going on to do a doctorate. Stymied, I wore pyjamas all day, read *La Morte d'Artur* while Craig left town for a teaching practicum.

I wrote a story casting Craig's flight from his family as an Arthurian quest. He figured in most of my work, usually prone with an arm over his eyes. He, on the other hand, couldn't wait to be employed, which is how we ended up within a year in a northern Alberta town where he'd landed a position as a high school teacher-librarian. Teaching jobs in the early eighties were hard to come by and only available to those willing to go afield.

What Craig and I had was as good a marriage as one can have given our incompatibilities. We both valued living in peace, neither of us disposed to fighting. We placed our children's well-being as top priority. We didn't, either of us, squander money or have unreasonable material expectations. We loved the same books and movies and cared about writing. We shared a political understanding. Why then do I say we weren't compatible? I failed Craig in two ways. He tried hard, but we didn't share a language in bed. The fact that he tried harder than I did was one of his lasting resentments. The other was his having to carry the financial load. Perhaps he felt misled. I had been ambitious at school and a high achiever. How did this not translate into the world of work? When either of us put a foot through a rotten floorboard, that board had been weakened by one of these fissures. We'd patch it over but were sure to tread too hard on the spots sooner or later. Craig could read me like a grade-school primer, but I didn't feel particularly recognized. It's entirely possible that this limitation was born of his illness, but I don't think so. There was something doggedly willful about the way he would not credit any part of me that didn't touch on him or on ours. The disappointments in our marriage were chronic rather than episodic. We papered them over with common interests.

The view back from the initially distant future shows how long it takes some of us to grow up. The birth of a child, or death or enfeeblement of a parent, may speed up maturity at any age. The death of a spouse only diminishes. The death of a spouse brings one as close to one's mortality as perhaps the death of a twin. At forty-six years of age, it felt as though I'd been robbed of the next thirty years of my life, rushed into retirement.

After Craig died, I joined a therapeutic 'grief group' for a few sessions. You do what you think you should to 'move forward' from an experience that is inherently unassimilable, indigestible. We think we can 'process' any hard stone ingested by the spirit and break it down in our systems with the aid of a digestive agent such as psychotherapy, but some experiences are not subject to absorption. In the group of eight people who had lost spouses in the preceding weeks or months, there was a woman a year into her mourning who had not moved a step beyond the shock of initial loss. She had been on a waiting list for a liver transplant, cared for in her precarious condition by her husband. The week she was finally scheduled for the operation, he was diagnosed with terminal brain cancer. She cancelled the transplant and stayed glued to his side during his frighteningly brief period of dying. She joined the group while recovering from the transplant and was still in it a year later. She hadn't paid a single bill, opened a single piece of mail, settled his estate, or cancelled his subscriptions since his death. He sat in his usual armchair with her daily. She poured his tea every morning and set a plate for him at each meal. He was there. She saw him, smelled him, felt his presence. Her mind told her he was dead, but her senses denied it.

The group leader suggested that I might benefit from helping this woman with some of her outstanding paperwork. We didn't live far from each other, and I seemed advanced in my handling of Craig's death. I had presented my state of mourning as having had a jump on it, as one might do preliminary readings over the summer for a course starting in September. I had been mourning the end of Craig for months before he died, while the disease ground away his ability to function in the world. I had been mourning the loss of my helpmeet and partner in life, the father of my children, the exceptional professional man, and kind, decent individual Craig had once had the capacity of being, the man he was. I thought I had a head start on my mourning. But you can't prepare for the finality of death. It is utterly incomprehensible, unabsorbable. You don't 'get over' it. At best, you form a containing seal around it like a tree does around a spike or axe blade lodged in its trunk. Within days, I had the first of a series of panic attacks.

For fifteen years after my husband took his life at the turn of the millennium, I wrote about our marriage. The book morphed through so many variations I lost track of stories like the forgotten names in an address book. At some point I stopped counting the ones tossed, the new hopefuls, an undulating tide. Words heaped upon words, stillbirths all, without a single breath of likeableness to animate the characters. Starting with Craig's first hospitalization in 1995, five years of repeated crises, most devastating for him, but also scarring for those of us around him, had knocked memory's kindness out of me. The problem was the book's premise. I saw us as a normal couple living a typical middle-class life, who happened to contend with the anomalies created by Craig's illness in a kind of sidebar to our main business of getting ahead and raising our kids. My aim was to show that we were a 'normal' family that had to cope with something that didn't necessarily detract from that state so much as attach to it. This may be the reason I ran into trouble. The half-animate creation fought back, refusing to live the lie.

The fragments of our marriage I've retained are the parts we never got right, bruises one can't help fingering, disfigurements that hurt to look at directly. Harder to hold in the heart is his dearness, a light radiating like his smile from behind the darkest clouds, transcendent and perishable. He took his own, his real story with him. What's left has become mine. As everything I turn my pen to, my story now rooted in a child raised by Holocaust survivors, the child who had to find a way to atone for the losses that led to her birth and who took too long to get there.

Easy to Love

ONE, CRAIG WAS ZACK'S FATHER. Two, he was a man with an edge even the six-foot, teenaged Zack didn't want to mess with, go up against. Father. Real good at things. Ran a big division at work. The ease with which he swung a racket, cut the ice on skates, curled his hands around a football. Born to it.

* * *

"Your Dad's a self-made man in every way. Baby, you don't know the half of it."

Drove Zack nuts what we left out when he was a kid. Background whisperings, the soundtrack of his childhood. It took a while to question what parents did, how they talked in low tones for hours on end. Maybe just like everyone else's. Or not. Not every mom liked to speechify. I'd launch, exhorting him to submit a piece to the school newspaper, train to be a lifeguard, his answer being to read the cereal box. All my bright ideas for everyone else. His dad lapped up my pep talks.

"You stay inside, Zack, and play with your little brother. Daddy and I are going for a walk." By the time Zack was ten, I'd leave Joshie at home with him while I took Craig out. Must have felt as though we were gone forever, but really just the time between lunch and dinner. Putting my apron down after cleaning up and then tying it again as soon as we came back in. The parent walks. Surely he eventually realized it was so as to take it outside, our whatever it was.

They'd had ten Lego wars during the time we were gone, Joshie announced. Setting up the basement afresh for each ambush. Joshie collecting yogurt containers, blocks, plastic bins, and marbles. Creating the whole intricate terrain, battle formations of two sides, and then all the skirmishes and engagements. The running play-by-play of Zack's commentary ten times over. Joshie picking up the dead guys, tidying the sets between scenes, clambering upstairs on short legs to fetch bananas and granola bars. It didn't sound as though they'd had a tough time. Zack preferred to be inside the cover of walls anyway, with his books and his toys, his brother the willing little gopher. No great hardship, but unaccountable.

Coming downstairs on a weekend morning to take his bowl of Cheerios in front of the TV. There we'd be, already at the table. His mom coaching his dad. "Lift the spoon. Now chew."

Had Zack heard correctly? Did he think his dad was sleep groggy; or that he himself was hearing things funny?

"Oh hi, Honey," I'd say brightly. "Daddy couldn't sleep in, so we're just getting a bite. Want me to take you a bowl down to the basement?"

His dad's breathing gulpy. Not acknowledging his son with a good morning or a had a good sleep? Nothing, as though the boy wasn't there.

These lapses must have seemed mysterious. Zack's talented father forgetting something as basic as feeding himself. Lingering on the basement stairs, listening for more than words, for breath that came raggedly or reassuringly even. Which it did in due course, the more his father swallowed.

My calling down so he'd get a move on, "Zachary, did you forget something?" Like maybe his real father.

Zack hadn't liked living in a house at first, even if it was just a block from the lake. Not as big a deal for him as it was for us, for his father who had craved being near water as long as I'd known him. In the apartment, everything had been just where Zack could reach it. In the house, he had to run up two flights for something he'd left in his bedroom.

That's where his brother came in. But when Zack was five, no brother yet, he hadn't liked the stairs; in fact, he hadn't liked being alone in the basement, not at the start. Thought the house wasn't such a hot idea. Or the deck with its wildlife—squirrels, cats, raccoons, worst of all, hornets. Give him a balcony above a sidewalk any old day.

Only Zack's father could lure him out. With a bat and a ball and a real leather glove just like his except small. Took him to the park on the lake. Threw the ball over and over, tosses that zeroed in on Zack's hitting zone. Even so, our boy swung full circle at times, which rankled.

"Too high, Dad. Dad, can't you see where I'm holding the bat? Daddy, throw them so I can hit them!"

His father winding up to make Zack feel he was getting a real hard one. Then pulling his arm back, levelling the poofy-perfect toss to the end of Zack's bat. Shouting, "Go, Zack, go!" And Zack throwing the bat wild, running the bases marked by their sweatshirts and a couple of shopping bags. A few whoops and high fives, and before he knew it, some pesky neighbourhood kids he didn't know, or ever wanted to, were asking to play. Zack hated that. Why should he share at bats? Let the other kids get their own dads. He didn't want to play a real game. He wanted all the turns, all the pitches to result in hits, all of Dad to himself. His father put up with it. No testy crack when Zack criticized a perfect pitch he'd missed. A polite brush-off for the kids who wanted in, although sometimes, he'd tell me afterwards, he made a suggestion: "No one lives in a world by himself. These boys look like they might know a thing or two about holding a bat. Let's have a little game."

Zack hadn't been able to argue without sounding like a brat. He didn't like making it seem it was all right with him when it wasn't, though. More often, he got his way. In Zack's eyes, his dad was the best. Good at throwing a ball, good at being patient, good at giving Zack what he wanted, making him feel that being with him was at the top of his dad's list. The kind of dad he'd choose if he got to pick. Who'd get so excited in front of the screen when they were watching the Canadiens, he slapped the floor with his palms and roared. The kind of dad who didn't get mad for no big reason like some, like his mom, for instance, who could have a hissy when Zack got red marker on a new pair of khakis. A father who wasn't petty or trivial, who didn't cheat or cut corners. Whatever he did, he did all out; whatever he was into it was at one hundred percent. A father easy to love.

* * *

"And what kind of a shot is that supposed to be?"

Riding with Craig in the ambulance later that night, I replayed the scene I'd pried out of Zack in fits and starts. Daring an over-the-shoulder glance at his father while scooping balls with his heel onto his racket. He was by the net, close enough to see his father's face, eyes shiny, skin red. They were just back from the beach after a four-hour drive, and it was still crazy hot. City hot that's not just blazing but thick. When his father had offered, "Let's go play," Zack had gone along with it because, one, his father was often away on business, and, two, there was something in his dad these days you weren't going to say no to. Zack couldn't put his finger on it, but it was there, like his dad was waiting for him to go ahead, just try it. So they were both out there panting in the hottest part of the day, the late afternoon sun drilling through their caps, and no swigs from the insulated jug could replenish the salt they had lost before even getting started.

Zack might have ignored the remark, but the tone hurt. Best not to answer. Just pick up the balls, and go back to the baseline.

"I've what, paid a fortune on lessons and you're still tossing the ball a foot in front of your face. Do that and it's going into the net guaranteed. Let's see it again."

Who needed this? Zack hadn't wanted to come out to play, anyway. You had to be nuts in this heat. Only his father. But it was his father, and he wasn't easy to go up against. Not even for his mother: "Today? In this heat? You know, Craig, you just started a new medication. Let's see how you take to it. Remember that time you passed out on the plane after switching meds?"

His father hadn't seemed to hear. Just barrelled on collecting tennis bags and checking the balls for bounce.

"Zack, we're going to need a tank of water. Your mother says it's hot." The tone.

I'd opened my mouth, then shut it. Zack must have stuffed down his misgivings, too. If I let them go, it had to be okay, right?

He tried again. Threw the ball above his head, but this time too high, racket funnelling air. Any athlete knew not to overthink it. Father bent at the waist, rocking his racket side to side, ready to pounce on the serve when it pounded over. If. Straightened, rubbed the soles of his Wilsons on the court surface to snuff out that last sorry attempt. Said nothing until he toed up a twig in disgust. "Again," he mouthed, a tight grimace. "You're going to practise that toss until each service finds the box."

Zack wanted to cry. It was ridiculous. Schooled like some little kid, which would have been worse, come to think of it.

"Look, Dad," he tried. Didn't want to start bawling, but. "Dad, maybe we should go home. I don't feel so hot."

"Oh, you want to throw in the towel just because someone's not stroking your ego, saying nice try son and all that crap. Well maybe a good try isn't always going to be good enough. Ever think of that? That maybe you should once in a blue moon, perish the thought, deliver."

Zack couldn't believe his ears. His father was a squeezed sponge oozing contempt. Was this what he really thought of his eldest? What he'd kept sucked in all along?

"Dad," he choked. What could he say to make it stop?

"Let's see just one half-decent serve, Christ, after years of lessons."

Language. It was usually Dad trying to clean the swearing out of his mom's. He'd been doing more of it.

"Daddy, you okay?"

His father whipped around, discharged a serve that kicked up dust inches from Zack's foot. Left a skid mark. Zachary startled in time to dodge another ball his father fired over. Had the presence of mind to run for the gate. His father stomped around picking up balls, stuffing them into his pockets. Didn't seem to notice Zack had gone outside the court. Assumed the stance in the other service box. Pummelled serves one after another until he ran out of balls. "See that! See that! You think you've got the picture yet?" Charging around to retrieve the dayglo orange and green and fuzzy duckling yellow missiles. Zack couldn't think what to do. What was best? He was losing his dad, his dad losing it.

Too far to run home, as they'd gotten to the court by car. Sweat drooling into Zack's eyes and rushing out hot. Afraid to say anything, not even *Daddy*. The balls pounding wild now, into the chain-link fence. His father hopping the net in this heat. How could he have the energy? Zack was fifteen and beat, dead, wasted. Pockets bulging, his father swung back to take the net again, and just like that, everything in the man crumbled. Cells and molecules separated, grains rolling into a heap.

Oh, God. Oh, God. Father down. Afraid to go near him. Afraid to leave him and run for help. Zack didn't decide, just found himself back inside the court. Knelt to check. His father's body curled like a bean. His Daddy making some kind of sound, words, once Zack got past the awful keening: "Sorry, Son. So, so sorry. Forgive me. Forgive me."

Zachary sobbed, "It's okay, Dad. I'm here. Daddy, it's okay."

His father didn't hear him, just repeated, "I'm so sorry, forgive me," in the high-pitched wail Zack had heard in newscasts from the other side of the world.

Zachary running. Out of the court. Onto the street. No one to be seen. Everyone inside where there was air conditioning. It was a hell zone, deserted, hot, unreal. He was running through it like you run in your nightmares. The kind of running towards something that keeps getting farther away. He'd never find a phone booth. He'd never be able to reach his mother. His father would die caged in some self-imposed prison of boxes and baselines and ground fault penalties. He ran with all the strength of his new-growth legs and lungs, the full power of his young heart, but he wasn't going to get where he'd thought he was going.

On August 1, 1999, we ran out of remissions.

All the King's Horses

S INCE WHEN HAS THE word 'enable,' which means to give power or opportunity to, or to make possible, taken on the suspicious cast of contemporary connotation? There were as many theories about my late husband's illness and possible treatments as there were doctors who assessed him. In due course, I was able to see their hospital notes, including the main diagnosis. 'Refractory' was the term used to describe his mental illness, defying effective treatment. And 'enabling' was the term for my role in it. Indeed, I had enabled much in Craig's life. I never had any doubt that the extent to which he was able to employ his gifts as a father and a publisher owed almost as much to my attention as to his diligence and creativity. But I stood accused of having fuelled the illness. I had resisted admitting that Craig's mental instability surpassed what we still thought of in the seventies and eighties as neurosis and that we now chalk up to chemistry. This helped him push through the hurdles his nagging and often morbid self-doubts threw up in his path. When he did not believe in himself, he could rely on me to cloak my confidence around his flayed self-image. He frequently worried at the wound of feeling like an imposter, his term. His accomplishments never spoke up for him against his sense of inadequacy. Most of us have an inner advocate who urges us to write that paper, take on a project, lead the team, or address an audience, because despite our anxieties, it believes that somehow we will manage. Craig took those leaps fully expecting to fall on his face. In holding the mirror to his successes, I became that missing faculty. In this respect, I protected him, not from the whole truth, but perhaps from an important part of it. He and I did not use the words 'sickness' or 'mental illness' ever. Perhaps this was why I stood accused of easing its progress.

My guilt may have lain elsewhere. A stubborn follower of the principles of psychotherapy, with a deep mistrust of the toxic effects of pharmaceuticals, for many years, I had stood in the way of chemical treatments for Craig's disorder. As a young spouse, I believed that time and love cure all. Perhaps if he'd had the benefit of drug therapy early enough, the neural pathways to depression and anxiety would not have worn as deep. This theory had been posed by a couple of his physicians. If they had started experimenting earlier with this anti-depressant or another, or that anti-psychotic which had to be introduced once the anti-depressants set off Craig's latent bipolar disorder, who knew how well or how long he could have continued to be as high functioning as he was almost to the end? We'd never have an answer. All I knew was that when I was requested to meet with the doctors after Craig's death, I didn't point a finger.

A triumvirate of specialists headed up Craig's hospital team: the pharmacological expert who weighed in on a consulting basis, the department head, and the rotating physician of the week. For over a decade, Craig had consulted a doctor who had supported him tirelessly in his hope for recovery. Eventually, as the illness gained possession of Craig's life, so did the hospital physicians. Each ward psychiatrist would start from the beginning. For both of us, it felt like stripping for a physical in front of a stranger on a weekly or biweekly basis over each eight-week stint of hospitalization. With each new staff, we bared our souls, hoping that some bit of previously overlooked data might be the key to reforming the refractory reprobate. Each ward physician felt some pressure to bring something new to the table.

The last one exuded a glowing vitality and confidence. It wasn't so much his striking well-being that felt like an affront, but the self-satisfaction with which he wore it. He might have shown compassion, I thought, by playing it down in his dress or posture or five o'clock shadow.

His supervisor, on the other hand, looked like a cute mouse, waving his furry paws apologetically when his hands were about to be tied by an administrative constraint: eight weeks of day programming; eight weeks tops for residential stay; eight weeks for recovery from electroshock treatment; eight weeks on the books before they cut their patient loose. "But I have children at home, and there are days when Craig has turned on us and I don't feel we're safe." Days, too, when he knew what he yearned to do and hated himself for it. My youngest on my lap, my hands over his ears, as from the basement, carried through the vents, we heard the sharp smacks, one cheek then the other, again and again, as Craig swatted helplessly at the poison within. Dr. Mouse usually caved, giving us a week's in-patient reprieve.

The ward doctor had smiled at me when he presented his game plan, assured of its welcome. After all, if not much could be done for the patient, at least the family's experience might be validated. Craig had to be encouraged to accept his condition as chronic, to understand that he would live the rest of his life as he had the last eighteen months, in terror and anguish, unable to function in the roles that gave him purpose: professional, father, husband, athlete. He should be made to understand that his expectations of us to relate to him as of old were onerous. At the same time, the pharmacological consultant came to the conclusion, albeit reluctantly as it risked another manic episode, that there was no recourse but to reintroduce an anti-depressant. The anti-psychotics after the last high had sent Craig into such a tailspin, as the specialist put it, "No human being should have to suffer such torment." This doctor would have looked at home in Silicon Valley. He wore plaid shirts and jeans, his straight hair shoulder-length. Once I noticed that his socks were mismatched. He was, however, precise and careful with his words. 'Suffer' and 'torment' megaphoned in my ears.

An incisive reasoner to the end, Craig understood very well what confronting his condition and accepting the limited terms of its contract meant: his prime years lived as a broken man, sidelined. Not an option for one who had been pivotal to the action in both the boardroom and on the playing field. The need for propulsion, that thing called 'drive,' had carried him from teaching to educational publishing, a love of books and ideas married to his undeniable urge to vie and succeed. Once the anti-depressant took effect, Craig was able to act on what he must have planned and played out in his head for weeks, always the strategist. It enabled him to uncurl from the fetal position that had become his habitual posture. With every last ounce of his courage and his strength, he ended his life.

I did not blame the staff psychiatrist, his shine rubbed off, tail tucked in, robust length slumped in a chair, so visibly punctured I might have felt sorry for him had feeling sorry for anyone in the world but my recently self-shattered Craig been, at that time, possible. His supervisor did the talking. I did not accuse any of them of miscalculation. Dr. Pharma offered his opinion humbly but firmly. He said they had more treatments in their repertoire, but in his opinion, Craig had a terminal form of the illness. He used the word 'terminal.' It was just a matter of time, he said, but the outcome would have been no different.

What is worse, enabling illness, or enabling death? What does enable even mean in face of the inevitable? The warty word splays over my frontal lobe like a toad.

* * *

The Craig I had married was bright, insightful, accomplished, and creative. He could be wickedly funny. He was, throughout his life, inordinately brave. As we say today of what we used to call growing up in an unhappy home, he was a victim of childhood trauma. From the moment I met him, I saw how he struggled. Yet, as he contended with his daily angsts, he built a rich life for himself that included higher education, mercurial professional advancement, and loving family life. He had infinite patience with our young sons. He fought for his staff against company policies that might further exploit their already-underpaid labour. He supported me so I might be free to stay home with the children and to write. A sweetness and fineness and generosity in Craig made up his essence. His smile could be disarmingly open, like a motion-activated floodlight surprising the dark.

The war against his condition was ultimately lost, but until the last years when Craig's illness gained like a malignancy that no surgery, chemo, or radiation could check, the myriad battles had gone our way. As John, my future husband, at that time my relation by marriage, had put it at Craig's memorial: "The illness stole the rest of his life, but it didn't steal the life he had." Craig had lived. He'd loved his kids, his work, his wife, his books, and he was very good at what he loved doing, including the sports he took to heart. By all measures we as a society assess lives as complete, Craig wrapped up his potential within forty-four years. What he had lacked was the ability to feel good about any of these successes or to believe that they would last.

It's hard knowing in your heart of hearts that you're glad to see the loved one go. Not glad that he had to go; that you cried against the stark injustice of. The main difference between my experience of the protracted final illness and that of the spouse of someone dying of terminal cancer is that I didn't know if there would ever be an end to the prolonged suffering of life outside the 'normal,' Craig's life in particular, but our family's too. Ahead were endless days Craig would not have considered even an existence, and no end in sight of his claims on me as wife. These were sentences in different purgatories, his, granted, much more like hell. The prospect withered my heart. I could never leave him in his desperate condition, but what was left of love beyond pity and compassion? In our mid-forties, neither of us could envisage a future. I didn't fail as his helpmeet, but rather in the lesser aim, after he died, to render our struggle in print. When the war is lost, all you can celebrate is that it's over.

With loss, you don't just mourn the one. I mourned the absence of the man I had nurtured for decades. I mourned the life gladdened by achievement and merit that he couldn't, but should have had. I mourned our marriage, fed by companionship, shared values, children, literature, and, yes, love based on all the above. I mourned the unblemished futures we had dreamed and worked hard to make possible for our sons. Never again would I catch the eye of the only other person on earth who could feel at the same moment the same joy in a being we had conjured together. I mourned how he would never know our sons' adult incarnations, nor they his pride in their consummation of growth. Everything that mattered I mourned, even as I was jolted free and clear, propelled onto the frighteningly blank slate of tomorrow.

* * *

What if the diagnostic report had read that in 'enabling' Craig's life in the main I had also, in a sense, opened the door wider to his illness; that the blessing of accomplishment came with a price? Would that not have been more true and less shameful? Medical practitioners are no less likely to err than the rest of us, but are more prone perhaps to deny it. Some situations, however, are inherently compromised. Illness and self-fulfillment walked hand in hand for Craig. He would have chosen self-realization and a short life any day over a prison term in limbo.

The shock and resultant shell shock weren't on account of Craig's death, but from the period that had led up to it. I had loved my husband and was infinitely relieved that he was gone. The latter phrase occluded the former on each page I wrote for over a decade. Not a single word of wonder about our resilience and mutual strength had found its way into the text, nor my unwavering hope. Nowhere did I draw a frame around two babes in the woods. A wood dark, gnarly, overgrown with nettles and briars. Never did I drop his hand until oh-so-near the end. We were walking on the boardwalk. It was early spring, one of the first days when the wind along the water blew warm. I must have known it, as I'd taken my jacket off. But I didn't feel it. I couldn't feel the inherent lightness of spring, the softness of the breeze, the tenderness of the leaves, the fecund smell of the air. I had turned off. Craig reached for my hand. I made a deadly error. I felt he was asking me for something, needing something again after I had already given for a quarter of a century more than I could be expected to give. The only time in our twenty-five years, I let go. He said, "Chief, can't you even take my hand?" A man who had thrived on giving himself. So he did.

Great Lake Water

WE WERE PACKED IN the beat-up suitcase we always took to the cottage. Commingling sands from past vacations had collected in its corners, dusting the neatly folded beach-wear. Each July, a few more grainy memories had found their way into the suitcase. Some of these had been preserved in snapshots, while others just rolled into the seams. Zack freeze-framed in his Paddington Bear rain hat, riding high in the baby backpack: an orange basketball stuffed in its net. Holiday bristle spiking Craig's family man like rum in nog. They looked sideways at the camera, the baby's wind-ruddied cheeks bouncing with Craig's tread. The camera saw the hank of lake-washed hair, the ironic cock of the head: me, he gestured, baby-whipped. But only the sand in the suitcase held the pressure of his fine soles, the authority of his spring into action at the annual ten-kilometre races held at the beach.

Lingering grains recalled Joshie splayed on the tennis court, his sandy slide miraculously cheating the ball of its down curve. For me, the few grains evoking that dive for the ball, a family legend, tacked it to eternity. Their cries in the pulsing waves, the boys and the man alternating head-first plunges into each racing crest. Me, bobbing up and down, tracking their heads through the foam of years. Half the lake bottom, it felt like, clumped from the crotch of my swimsuit onto the bathroom tile, but a few specks clung to the Lycra like sugar on a licked spoon. Grains of sand like moments in time I mustn't allow to dissolve.

The jelly candy-coloured noodle was an afterthought jammed under the trunk lid. Josh, these days, required a football or glove and ball or soccer ball on the beach. Preferred his bare hand to a shovel when dredging wells to other seasons beneath the baked surface of the sand. Zack would bury himself for hours with his book under an Arabian drapery of towels and shirts. He'd use the noodle to swat at always one errant gull, spottier than the rest, beadily tenacious. Zack, sixteen, over six feet, who would also assume the front seat, while the ten-year-old wedged against an outsized camp bag strapped like a dummy big brother into the middle seat belt. The orange cooler, a prayer stool for his feet. The car, packed for more than three. Others would come up later, cousins, wispy-bearded youths. Me, as den mother to ensure they didn't drown in alcohol or from it. Joshie and I checking out all dealers in ice cream. Days filled with— instead of to—distraction. The box that was Craig would fit where?

* * *

The previous May, when the whole family had gathered under our roof, Elaine's voice was much quieter than usual. What models of control we'd all tried to display for the children's sake. Josh's face screamed orange and black and yellow with the grease paint his best friend, Sam, had used to transform him into a tiger. They roared around the house as though the word that was like a thud in the head had never been uttered, as though he'd never woken in the basement the evening after his birthday sleepover. Voices and steps overhead. He had ascended the stairs into sudden quiet. Me, no doubt looking like my juices had been sucked out. The too many bodies melting away so it was just us two. And I'd strung together words that didn't make sense to him. The house didn't make sense. All those people gathering after his birthday party was over. Too quiet for that many. And the words I'd put together too carefully, each separate and flat, had not inflated with any meaning. Except, finally, one.

Sammy's mom had flown in like the good witch, all crushed velvet and red hair and smelling of what Josh called 'achou-ie' like she'd sneezed.

Swept him away from the unnatural quiet in a bright puff of smoke. *Presto magico*, the house had disappeared. The too quiet, too busy, colourless rooms gone. My face so dry it could crack, gone. His father, Craig, gone.

When she brought the boys back a couple of days later, Josh the tiger and Sam purple-pink on his heels, they crashed into the house hilariously, still partying on. They had to pull up short. Josh had forgotten. Still here, the too-full rooms. And when had his aunt Elaine ever spoken in measured tones? "What do you mean, go by yourself?" she was saying when Josh interrupted her.

"Where to?" he shouted.

Everyone looked at the two little boy-animals arrived from another dimension. No one wanted to shift their gears.

"Well," I answered Elaine as carefully, "I'm not taking the kids."

"Maybe not the kids but also not alone." Elaine more insistent.

My glance: *back off.*

Then to Joshie, "Hey, Kiddo. There's lots of good food in the kitchen. Why don't you get Sammy something to eat?"

Josh turned from me for a cue from Zack, sleep-bleary at midday, pausing on each step down from the second floor as though pushing into cold water. "Montreal bagels," he grunted.

Aunt Elaine, Zachary liked to say, maven of all.

"Yeah, so where?" My baby boy's sneer hit hard. Planted in the middle of the living room, I felt like a buffeted signpost loosed from its moorings. Zack looked like he needed to kick something. He shoved towards the kitchen.

"Zachary, please. She's just a tad big-sister bossy." I couldn't help using the sad-strained smile he could do without.

Elaine swallowed back whatever she'd been going to say. But she would not let me go there alone. Who did that? In her view, there were reasons for most customs, based on common sense. Others had been in this foreign landscape where we were now lost and rudderless. Traditions towed one in. Okay, not with the kids or the oldsters. So then with whom? A sister's place. I could almost see the words floating up unbidden. You're canvassing for a worthy cause, when a door flings open on someone you've seen before. Maybe he cleaned your gutters or served you at the bank, but there he stands unshaven, in undershorts at midday, an unbidden revelation.

* * *

We two sisters stood beside the coffin in a room that was too hot and dry for century-old stone walls. An unholy conversion of a stone chapel, steepled, picturesque, with a backroom furnace for transforming DNA. Or does that stay fixed, imprinted even in ash?

Elaine and I were the same height. People claimed we look alike. Craig said he never saw it. Two small, dark-haired women a stranger might mistake for the other. Elaine in glasses, not an occasion for vanity. I wore dress pants, a silk blouse. The ones I'd worn to Christmas parties. I didn't want Elaine to touch me. I thought that's what I didn't want. What I wanted was to run my hands along it, feel the hot air already in its sides. I wanted to be alone. Maybe. Shrank from any finality. We stood, sisters, making it up as we went. Tears poured dryly from just the eyes. Elaine's or mine? I decided Elaine's. Elaine's shoulders shook. Elaine was capable of heaving sobs. On the phone when I'd told her, she'd wailed. As she had when our father died, too. My sin of pride is understatement. The ironic remove. Holding the phone waiting to take my place at bat. Waiting for my turn that, surely, had arrived, however long it took Elaine to wear out the pitcher. My waiting silence was sarcastic, petty. To begrudge a person her grief, Craig his due, someone tearing at her breast. Instead, this guarded composure. I put both palms on the box while Elaine wept. The only proof was a stained wedding ring the officer had handed me in a Ziploc baggie. My hands adhered to the thrum of the conveyor belt. I hadn't touched him for so long. A motor cranked, though none of it felt possible, certainly not the quickening pulse of the coffin. As it moved forward, it ran beneath my palms, guiding me as one might a pencil hand through its first letters.

We walked. A green churchyard in the centre of the city. The stillness converted surrounding traffic to an insect drone. You couldn't just jump back in the car. We went through the story again that had been gone over many times. Who says I didn't get my turn? Some graves went back two centuries, spilled down the hillside onto the road that once had been fields or woodland. Elaine was careful. It wasn't what she did or didn't say that felt like a gift but that she so obviously wished to find the right thing that would work for me. I took it. I took the arm that was offered, and we strolled, two peas in a pod.

Later, I reviewed: I ate capers and smoked salmon on a bed of greens. Lengths of baguette on the side. Elaine saying I had to eat to keep up my strength. If not then, when would I get a pass on fortitude? A coral reef on my plate. Wedges of red, pools of pale cucumber. Capers dark tears on pink flesh. Let the salmon weep. I believed I was done. For months, in the basement on the floor where no one could hear. I believed I'd had a head start on the whole business, could miss a drop or two now. Thanks, I'd pass, but feel free to carry on, I tipped my head to the salmon. I believed I'd wept enough, over a year of it, into pillows and dish towels, behind dark glasses in the supermarket where it came on because a cart had raked my heel. The coarse wool of a winter coat sleeve, the closest thing to a caress as I swiped away snot. I'd wept it all out, so I thought. Sliced the lettuce into neat mouthfuls. Incorporating the unthinkable with every bite. Kept it all down, another hard new fact of existence.

The day after he'd died, I'd woken early. A sleeper in every bed. In Zack's room, two large lengths in addition to his. Not a night would he be left on his own, but some Douglas fir-sized friend would be there, not planned but in seamless succession. Josh being at Sammy's allowed room in his bunk for Elaine's grown daughters. Elaine and our mother in the basement. Our father's cousin, Zsuzsa, in the living room. I was finally back in my bed after months of fluttering moth-like in the night. I had changed the sheets sometime in the night before I could lie on them. And up again at dawn, the house breathing damply with their sleep. Elaine had said maybe the air conditioning should be turned on.

She expected drop-ins. Expected? I felt paused. I was suspended in that gap a stopwatch leaves between the off and the back on, that place above the line of text inserted with a caret.

At dawn I went out onto the deck. Overnight, the earth had awoken. The lilacs were out, emitting their first heavy scent in the dewy mist, the garden sprung into leaf. An image returned from the Whitman poem about the presidential hearse's progress through the countryside, lilacs opening at its passage. The garden descended in tiers of wavering greens. Oaks at the bottom swayed with the rising chorus of spring birds happy to be back, to be there on a glorious May morning.

I leaned on the deck rail pressing hard into my rib cage, it hurt that much, the early lime wash of the spirea, and a breeze so suddenly mild I could stand outside in pyjamas. A house filled to bursting with loved ones, lilacs busted out. The bitter, bitter beauty of this release back into life. Movement shook the bushes at the foot of the hill, called to me, then separated from the leaves in a flush of red winging higher and higher. Don't go. It revealed itself as it flew. Bloodied, beautiful. Not so fast. It became a distant fleck and melted into foliage. Hanging behind it in the air were the words he left without saying: I'm not mad. A raw, lucid cry of what he still possessed and was able to give. Thank you had yet to stab like this.

* * *

July heat. Before setting out for the drive to the beach, I opened all four doors to cool off the interior. A honeyed temperature, viscous and yellow. As July as it could get. It had been July for more than two months, almost like July back then in May, each day an offering of colour and light. I could see how myths of sacrifice take hold, a life offered up in exchange for some necessary restoration of peace or order.

I turned back to the house to round up the kids. The storm door's handle burned my fingers. It clapped behind me, a rattle of glass thinly cased in aluminum. I pulled the inner door shut to keep out the sun's flame, had to blink a few times to clear the glare, and shouted while my eyes adjusted, "You guys ready?"

His outline was right there just a few feet away. I startled. The form filled in long and dark and mop-headed. Zack cradling the box in his big-boned forearms. His father's bones held by his father's bones. Irresolute and certain at once. Standing there like now what? Yet he grasped the box with such familiarity, the winch in my chest tightened. He held it without compunction as though it were part of him, pushed into his shoes without giving it up. Zachary, I wanted to say, forgive me. A parental reflex.

"I'll take that," I offered, not expecting an answer.

It hadn't felt fair to drag Elaine back with me to the cemetery. Not Elaine's trouble. Mine to thrash through, ford across, ours.

* * *

The midday light had striped across Zack's prone back. A breeze swelled the thin silk curtains, gentling his bare skin. The bed dipped as I sat beside him. My fingers tugging lightly at his tangles. He let them study his scalp, a mother's rippling affection. Another body stirred on the cot. Which friend? Who's there? Who wasn't, rushed back in.

"It's after noon, Zack. Come with me to get your father."

All the times in the last year and a half that I'd asked, "You want to come with me to see your father? Shall we stop in on the way home to pick up Daddy's laundry?" Once there, in the parking lot beside the brick low-rise wing resembling public housing, I'd glanced at the windows that no one ever looked out of. Striped hospital curtains closed against the loveliest of days. A couple of patients out back smoking, even when it rained, the puddles when I excused myself as I passed by them, clogged with butts. I'd turned to Zack who had already assumed the front passenger seat, come to think of it, "Are you coming in?" I hadn't pressed him. He was a boy. He hadn't wanted to see his father there. If Craig wasn't home, Zack could pretend he was on business. He was in

Vancouver or St. John's. He was in Tokyo, New Zealand, or Cincinnati. He was in San Diego.

His father was often away, not gone like these people on the ward. His father had a home and a profession. He was able. And he would get better. Zack would wait.

This time I didn't ask. When I stood, the bed rocked. "Don't take too long," I said, running a knuckle up the cheek still soft beneath its first beard.

* * *

Alongside, but above the cemetery, the subway exploded from the ground like a geyser spewing its length into a silver river. On school days, Zack would rock and doze in the early morning or sway from an overhead bar on the way back, paperback held close to the nose. One didn't feel hurled through distance until the train broke out of the depths, churning, clawing for air over the valley. The sky, a sudden slap of light against dopey lids. The glint of cars on the highway below, and a thread of river wending lakewards. He hadn't realized it was there, a green silence within the city's thudding heart, a parenthetical aside along the rattling subway sentence that ground into Castle Frank station. I told him the cemetery was quite old. Hadn't his class toured the city's historical sites in grade ten? Yes, but.

"I didn't know it was here either," I said. Almost twenty years in this city, and I drove by it whenever I went downtown.

"You've got to be a pedestrian and transit user to know a place intimately. The way I used to know Montreal," I added.

Zack would never again look up blinking from his book to wonder at the subway blundering blindly out of the ground. Instead, his neck would tense to the smack of light.

We turned left. And quickly left again into the grounds fenced from the street by a brace of evergreens and wrought-iron gates. A churchyard was all people were supposed to think.

"So where is it?"

I pointed out the old stone gatehouse. A discreet sign, white lettering on black, read OFFICE.

"Nah, that couldn't, it's too small."

Oh, he wanted to know where the metamorphosis had taken place. See the pretty steepled church? Not your typical furnace room in the back. I held the soft sell, the lie, in contempt.

Nothing sacred about the destruction of a body. Without a body, Craig was gone. There'd been people yesterday in the chapel up front, praying their private invocations in an alternate universe while Craig's DNA disassembled.

"You know, Aunt Elaine and I took a walk here yesterday. She liked the old headstones."

What I tried to screen out. He wouldn't rise to that bait, although with Zack a bit of historicity could go far, sucker that he was for the past. He was what, a two-year-old I thought I was going to distract with "ooh, look at the choo-choo"?

"You know, Mom, where they did it."

Zack wasn't about to step into that church, though. His father had hated churches, hated the whole business, which was why we weren't putting him in the ground. The only one who had cried at his great-grandmother's funeral, Craig's family used to say. Because, Craig admitted, he was scared to death among the graves. Zack's father hadn't been altogether gone, not as an anxious boy nor as a man in a hopeless situation. Craig had taken his illness below stairs to the basement so that Zack and Josh wouldn't have to see it, although of course, they heard, you couldn't not hear, and Craig, far enough gone to not realize it. All of us were only now understanding the word's implacable meaning.

He let me steer him by the elbow: "Zack?"

"Fucking quiet, don't people work here with shovels and backhoes and lawn tractors?"

Someone had to stoke the furnace or run it. Others must keep records. They had to package the stuff.

"All too fucking quiet and discreet and considerate. It's a fucking place of business after all. Why can't we hear a voice?"

Three desks behind a counter. That musty, old-fashioned office smell from when files were still on paper, although the room was surprisingly light as if freshly refurbished. A slim man in a short-sleeved dress shirt rose to serve us. Zack must have realized I'd been holding his hand because he dropped it when I asked for Craig by name.

Like a check claim for lost luggage. You walk up to a counter, say a name, Zack's father's.

"Of course, I'll be right back," said the man in the sports shirt as though someone were sleeping, we were both sleeping, sleepwalking through these motions, as the short-sleeved man was too aware, he'd seen so many like us going through the necessary paces in some kind of trance we shouldn't be startled from. Not here in this public place where the stranger with the bare, sparsely haired arms would have to comfort? Restrain? Occupational hazards. Bad day, he'd say at home, unbuttoning the top button of the pale blue shirt.

We waited in the unnervingly calm facade. We were Fabergé eggs supposed to support each other when it was excruciatingly impossible not to let the other drop.

"Here," Zack said, "I'll take it."

The man walked to the end of the counter carrying the box in two hands. He unlatched the swing gate and came over to our side. Zack held out his arms for the package as though this was why he'd been put on earth. This was what it had all been for, the growing, the learning from powdery bald babyhood to bristling youth, for this culminating moment when his strong, young wrists bent with a weight that surprised. He hugged it to his chest. His. His father. More diminished than he was by the illness that had ravaged his mind. That was merely figurative. This was it, ultimately reduced. Some thing still, a physical vestige of Daddy that Zack could hold on to.

My son, frozen in the unnatural embrace, wrists curled lovingly around the sharp corners of the box. I got why nature prefers curves.

I slipped a steadying arm around his waist to guide him along. One size-thirteen baby step after the other. The braveness between us but a film. I didn't know yet that the box weighed what Zack had when the surgeon had cut him from my belly and placed him, gummy-blooded, pendant, into his father's arms. Craig's long face—the exhausted eyes, gouged cheeks, chin as keen-edged and square as if it had been levelled—had filled with his son's first inhalations. As the anaesthetic's black tide swept over me, I noted how life is indeed mutually given.

Mother and son, we took our steps together to the car. The man behind the counter may have watched us through a window. A small woman and a big boy, much taller than the short-sleeved man for whom the box wasn't even a momentary burden. We leaned on each other gingerly so as not to pull the stitches.

* * *

Each day, after bringing his father home in a box, Zack walked downstairs to be dinged right between the eyes. He paused on the same step and looked up into the book nook where Zack had put him. As though no one would notice Craig there among his beloved books. A fly on the wall.

"He didn't wait for me," he had cried initially. "He didn't hang around long enough to see how I'd turn out." Perhaps that was Zack's flinty rejoinder whenever the box dinged him first. Each time Zack came down for breakfast, 'Don't forget me' came to mind as though neon-markered across the neutral package wrap like any parcel come by mail.

I watched Zack hover on the stair, delivering some mental harangue at the start of his day. "Like right. Won't see how I turn out. Joshie, athletic wunderkind—soccer-baseball-long-distance-running-tennis star. Nothing he couldn't do, the baby genius. Little perfect-pitched maestro. Never know what I might be capable of, though. Joshie your mirror image, but I was the surprise at the bottom of the crackerjack box you didn't bother to finish." A one-sided rant until he realized he was communing with a box, and took the bottom stairs in one bound. Stuffed it all down with cereal in juice, the same lactose-free breakfast his father in his sufferance had put up with for decades.

"Oh my God. Just like Craig. Bent over the bowl like that, and when he turned to me, for an instant, the spitting image. More so since." Elaine's voice carrying even when she thought she was out of earshot. Some comfort, though. Zack was taller than his father had been. He had my white, unblemished skin, my father's eyes, Elaine's full-lipped mouth. But physically cast in his father's mould.

"The way he moves, that tender inclination towards the person he's speaking to—" A catch in Elaine's throat cut her off.

Well, it was nice of her to say, although I had let out that air-from-a-tire noise. Zack looked up at me as though to say, "What, you're going to give out now? Fall apart? Sorry, Dad used up those chits." It was true, all that were left were the hang in, hang on, don't hang up kind. What I was stuck with.

Zack was stuck with having known. The moment the officer had stepped into the living room.

The dark uniform drawing everything into it, the light from the front windows, Joshie's piano stool and ivory keys, the pictures on the walls of the covers of his father's books, the pine bookshelves and leather sofa, the whole exposed brick wall of family photos: Josh and Zack as babies, me and Elaine making faces at each other long before we had kids, Craig running into the finish of one of his million races. The officer had expanded, filling the room with an obliterating blackness, hat in hand. Zack must have known, although I said quickly, "Go downstairs, Sweetie. Right now." He flew, too, relieved to get to be the child just a little longer. Get to see his mother one last time as small, but strong, knowing what was necessary, what was best. Stepping up to the plate with resolve. Go ahead, officer, take your best shot. Zack must have known. He wanted protection from the truth, but he knew. Joshie passed out on the basement futon after his birthday all-nighter, video game flashing on the computer. I heard Zack's fingers click the controls hoping to drown out the faint murmur of our voices, the officer's and mine, until he couldn't stand to wait any longer. This was Zack's house too, Zack's life, Zack's father. He must have known, but couldn't bring himself to. He'd known, but would wait to be told until he couldn't wait another moment. Swallowed the stairs in two strides. The policeman in the armchair fingering the rim of his hat band. Me on the edge of the piano stool, back straight. Both of us turned to the boy instantly. And I was holding on, holding him together. Neither of us remember the officer leaving, only the room back, its furniture there, where it was once, but no longer in place. My arms pressing around him. "I'm sorry, Baby. I'm so sorry, Baby. Forgive me for telling you. I'm so very, very sorry."

My compass had always been to get the kids over. Even if the only way was by balancing on water. They didn't have to know it. I could paint them a path, let it unroll, say see you on the other side, strike out like it was easy as pie. It was all in the example. You didn't plan it. You followed an internal compass. Later, people would say there were other ways. Everyone had a notion of how others should navigate. But I was in it, sinking fast. I thought of my kids and turned my face upwards. Bubbles rising. "He will get better," floated up inside me, lifted me like a balloon. They said you should tell them, "Your father's a sick man. He loves you but his sickness gets in the way." But I said, "Your dad will get better, go on with your lives. He'll catch up." And little ducks in a row, they put their feet one after another on rime as thin as membrane.

Zack was certain I was holding him that tight so he wouldn't see right away how everything had changed. Later that night, he told me he thought everything must be over. No more English compositions or chemistry labs or history assignments. Over. He saw a chasm open in the floor of the living room, and we tottered on the edge of it, he, and I, and the party-sleeping-off baby of the family. He saw his future topple into it, university, summer travel, learning to drive, his father sitting through three endless hours of Zack's convocation. And nothing left on the edge but the residue of what we once had aspired to. All altered by this unassimilable given.

And there it was up in the book nook, taking everything in—Zack's sullen mien; Elaine's consoling observations; my dazed, pushed-over will; Joshie's oblivious, denying ebullience; and Grandma's, yes, the Holocaust-surviving, three-husbands-buried, matriarch's defeat by a sink full of dishes. The whole fucking mess of us.

Zack had taken in something too. With each hard mouthful of cereal the juice couldn't mitigate. If he was like, he was a living testament, right? He wouldn't have to always remember.

* * *

The house was full all that first week. People came before work, after work. I opened the front door to get the paper, found a casserole dish, note taped to the side. Some couldn't bring themselves to face the boys. A plastic ice-cream bucket of home-made cookies materialized between the doors. One tall friend, elegant in work clothes, was in the kitchen cleaning out the freezer that had chosen to stage a breakdown. I wished. The friend arrived on her way to work with bagels and four flavours of cream cheese; instead rolled up her sleeves, slapped on rubber gloves. I wondered at her energy. My eighty-year-old mother at the sink insisted on hand-washing the dishes, although the dishwasher was only half-stacked. I couldn't muster the energy to protest. Why was someone always peeling carrots, chopping, slicing? Four friends from the kids' old alternative school were unpacking muffins. One broke off a piece and pushed it in my mouth. "Are you eating?" she asked, and everyone laughed. Frozen food piled next to the unloaded freezer, the counter overflowing with vegetables. Breads, bagels, baked goods, we could have opened a business. People in and out all day, we had to be prepared to feed them, someone said, maybe Mummy lifting her eyes from the suds in the sink and blinking at the new leaves beyond the window as though for the first time. When had she become Mummy again instead of Grandma? The Mummy of us all, waving a half-washed plate under the tap.

"Look," I whispered peevishly, and a friend bent down, "she barely introduces the plate to the water."

Newly minted widowhood accounted for only part of my bitchiness.

If it wasn't the doorbell, it was the telephone, and if I had to smell another lily I'd choke. Mercifully, it was warm enough to put them out on the deck. My cousin's husband John arrived straight from the airport, still in his suit, a briefcase, and garment bag dumped in the coatroom. He came directly towards me extending his hands, led me outside for a word in private, and I cast about for something to say that I hadn't said already a million times to the other voices on the phone, to the intent, considerate faces around the table. Because he'd dropped everything to be here and I wanted to return the kindness by putting it to good use. We faced each other on kitchen chairs. No one had thought yet to bring the lawn furniture out of storage. He held my hands in, I saw, his very large ones. I noticed as I didn't remember registering quite like this before, how big a man he'd turned into. Once, he and Craig were both tall and thin and boyishly gangly, John loose-jointed compared to Craig's taut musculature. Their talk springing between topics, elastic as their treads along the boardwalk by the lake. Then came the kids' birthdays, Craig ever more chiselled and pared back, John progressively padded. Conversation attenuated over time. Why was that? Craig and I hunkered down to weather our gathering storm, all hatches battened. Yet here was John, as of old, holding my hands, regarding me as though I were fragile, precious, like he'd never seen me before. I felt nothing at that moment mattered more to him, not even his children who had just stepped out to pick up paper plates and napkins for the memorial din- ner, not the discomfiting presence of his estranged wife as she screened calls so I might have time with him uninterrupted, not the work he had left behind precipitously on another continent, or the house full of guests he had yet to meet, than I alone in my need. I froze, caught in the concentrated glare of kindness. Feeling utterly looked after, I was tempted to drop it all, the strength, the guard. Oh, to let it all slip off and stand naked, defenceless, forlorn, just to be taken care of. How big he'd grown. Moving across the living room, he had sailed in like a ship, belly-led in his steel grey suit, solid, unsinkable. I was suddenly dry of all syllables. What opened was behind the eyes. An eye-thing disconnected from that wallop between my ribs in the night or wrung at other times by the crank in the same cavity winding ever tighter. Detached from any pressure in head or heart, it was a grain of grit behind the lids. I sat there spilling as he crushed my fingers, a welcome contraction.

* * *

"Get in." I held the car door open. Josh was already stuffed into the back. He punched a hollow in the side of the duffel bag to rest his head for the long drive to the beach. The youngest got the comfort shaft, but there was pride in not whining. Zack carried the box like it was glass, but it was more like the box Josh's pair of size-five tennis shoes had come in. Made as little sense as anything, your brother carrying your father in a shoe box to his favourite place on the planet.

Joshie had seen it all and decided he didn't have to look at everything close up. Zack had gotten away to school. To sleepovers. Zack had been old enough to fly to Vancouver, New Hampshire, and Chicago; his best friend's banker dad had kept getting transferred. Then there'd been high school trips to New York, Boston, and London. Zack had missed scenes that Joshie couldn't. The slow, shambling steps that would sometimes stop in the hospital corridor in front of him, so out-of-place, a child, and stare milkily or make an incomplete gesture. I said hello, then touched Josh on the back to move on. He could speak for himself, said hi, turned on his own condoling smile, not much different from his manner towards my mother and the old aunties and anyone else he had no intention of letting in. Through open doors, he saw people lying fully clothed on their beds. His father's would be closed, and we'd knock before entering. Craig raised himself blearily, hair flattened on one side, puffy and sticking up on the other because he'd laid on it wet, no sooner than he'd washed and dressed. "Hey, Pumpkin," he exclaimed, not falsely cheerful—he was always delighted to see Josh—but like it was hard work. His father with a comatose stranger in the next bed, when he could have been home sleeping next to his mother. It wasn't like what he had was contagious, wasn't like he had the kind of illness Josh imagined could kill you. That's the thing Josh had needed to know, needed to stick his nose right up against because when he knew that, everything else made its own misaligned meaning. Exactly how? And when? And why? Why *then* when just that morning, Josh had come up from the basement to get his Magic cards and there was his father eating pancakes? A man who could eat and talk and walk and on good days read the newspaper. No matter what I said, sitting Josh down on the sofa. "Something bad has happened." Dead?

Josh's father had just gone for a walk after a pancake breakfast. Was there something Josh had not understood about the word 'dead'? Did it have more than the one meaning? It must have seemed something like that to him when I said, "The illness killed your father." "I don't get it. What do you mean?" I had looked over at the score on the piano, "Mission Impossible." Josh had just about nailed it for his recital. "Oh, Joshie," I'd cried, "you don't need the details. Zack doesn't want them. The point is Daddy's gone, he has no more life, he's dead because of that terrible illness." But Josh couldn't wrap his head around it.

His father bent low over a plate of leftover pancakes from Joshie's birthday breakfast. Just the night before, his father had come to the play of Jacob Two-Two with him and his mother and Sammy and the others. His father hadn't looked worse than usual, just had that meek, spacey look that wasn't Josh's real Dad. "How exactly? How come? I don't get it," said Josh. "You need to tell me." Joshie stepping off the wide-swathed path blazed by his brother. Joshie cutting through the thicket on his own. If it made my face crumble, he couldn't help it. That was one of the new things he tried not to notice.

* * *

"Put it on the floor," I said, "it's heavy."

Zack didn't bother to answer. Made no motion to relieve himself of the package. Stared absently through the car window at the neighbour's yard where a tattered Canada Day flag fanned the heat. Someone from one of the cars that pulled up regularly to deliver groceries put the flag up a few summers back; no one had bothered to take it down. The neighbours were elderly. Old. Ancient. He and Josh had both knocked their front teeth out before they reached kindergarten. Strange coincidence. Ran in the family. Craig had knocked his out as a kid playing hockey. I'd say I didn't see how other people's kids held on to all their teeth; ours weren't the only ones to have ridden wheelie toys on the sidewalk or climbed a slide in the park. Staring at the tattered flag, Zack demanded to know how other people managed to live as long as the neighbours.

"Hey," chirped Joshie, "we going to stop for lunch on the way like usual?"

"Right, like anything's usual. Like we're going to order Dad's mushroom burger, hold the ketchup and mayo, like usual."

"Sure, Sweetie," I tried smoothing things over. "You want to choose the first tape?"

Zack seethed silently. But Zack was so vocal, as loud, no way louder, than his aunt Elaine. You could just about hear even what he was thinking. Like we were just going to the beach. The car packed for the annual pilgrimage to wind and sand and firestorm skies. Like we were going to fucking play Hearts without Craig's scathing indictment of my useless strategizing after all these years. We were going to ride the waves without hearing his whoops. We were going to eat his maple sandwich cookies and beat each other at tennis instead of losing to him. We were going to have fucking fun in the sun. Is that what Josh and I were suggesting? Yet it was more unthinkable to never go there again. "Someone should tear the fucking rag out of the tree. It's an insult to the nation!" he finally erupted.

I pushed in the tape Josh handed over the seat. Familiar strains of rock and roll after my time. My head too full of anxious static in the last years to keep track of the new groups. "Which one's this again, Counting Crows?"

"Ah, Mom, how come we still have to tell you?" The little one relentlessly chipper. I played dumb adult, pitifully out of it. "I can't keep them straight from The Hip."

"That's fucking ridiculous." Zack burned. "You'd have to be tone deaf." The weight of it sank in his lap.

Yesterday, pillows and sheets in my arms, on the way to stuff the duffel bag. I loved the feel of it, the clean softness of bedding, linens, the billowy baggage safe enough to cushion against Joshie in the car. Spotted the box over the top of my laden arms as I went downstairs. Must do something about. Unlike Zack, I needed a stool to reach up. Wobbled under the load, one leg probing the air for purchase. Vows made when you're too young to realize what you're promising and you find yourself on the floor beside a thin-legged stool, lifting a parcel up and down because you can't open it or leave it alone. He weighed a hundred and fifty-five pounds as an eighteen-year-old boy when we moved in together, not even ten pounds more when he ran long distance in his thirties. The meds made him pack on another twenty in the last year; it wouldn't have happened otherwise, what with the sports and a moderate appetite. Now this, a small, dense package. I put it on the bathroom scale. A good-sized birth weight, like his sons. I thought, do it now, before. I plunked myself where I was, the upstairs hallway between the bedrooms, and realized it was the only place it would have been possible. What I intended was to unwrap and find, leaving no trace of my passage. It seemed of utmost importance not to alter anything in the packaging, as if after such ultimate reduction and transformation, not a scrap more change could be withstood. By whom? I ran a finger lightly over the white-labelled name, lifted the tape on one end without tearing the paper, and worked my way around carefully. That's it, you just had to pick the box up again, one skin thinner, slide the wrapper out from under, put it an arm's length away, no rips, no folds, no crinkles. Confront the corrugated cardboard within. Look for the openings without laying a finger, then slip a pinky into each end, and release the tucked-in flaps. Dread, resignation. I'd heard plenty about human ash, a buzzword of family history.

* * *

"You're not going to bury!" my mother had pleaded back in May. "How can you burn when they were all burned, your grandparents and aunts and cousins, your own half-sister. Jews don't burn their dead, never, not before the war, and even more not after. Have you no sense of where you belong?"

"But Craig wasn't Jewish. He was frightened of graveyards."

"Not Jewish! He was a son to me!"

The plate had waved vaguely everywhere except in the suds or under the running water.

For a moment I had thought my mother would raise it in front of the window like a pagan offering, or over the kitchen tile to smash in memory of the destruction of the Temple, or place it butter-smeared and encrusted with bagel seeds against her face and mash her features into it.

"Ma," I'd said sharply.

My mother had wavered at the sink. She'd forgotten where she was, at home in her own kitchen or mine or Elaine's or the one where she grew up vying for even the tantalizing aromas with six other siblings. She could have been starved and tearing the ground for roots in a war-torn landscape she was so displaced in the moment by loss. Hand trembling under the weight of the china, she turned in the direction of the familiar admonishing voice, found her youngest daughter's face. Must be disorienting to see your baby middle-aged, in mourning! No doubt the mourning showed in the tight lines around my mouth, something unfocused in my eyes that darted around the kitchen unable to light on a soothing image. She'd regarded the plate in her shaking hand like a miracle pulled from drowning waters, gripped her wrist with the other, and guided the plate to a safe landing in the drain board.

"Platonically sanitized," I, the younger widow, had muttered.

* * *

I owed it to someone to confront the ash. I had to handle the cardboard gently so nothing flew out, but as I lifted the flap to peek, there was yet another box of hard plastic that I turned over and back, and on its side, but found no means of entry. Are you or aren't you supposed to? I was loathe to even scratch the surface, let alone pry the lid off with a knife, but it didn't come to that. I'd just been too agitated to notice the edge that suddenly presented. One end flicked up with a fingernail. And in there? A thick, clear plastic bag twist-tied shut. I pulled it forth. Twist-tied like fruit from the market, like grain, a whole grain from the health food shop, all ten pounds of what was left twist-tied and altogether too easy to open.

You can't, but you did. Untwisted the tie that separated you from impossible. Placed the precious strip of wire among the other valuables so all could be perfectly restored. And inserted my hand. Annihilating intimacy. I had felt the pressure of the obstetrician's hands on my uterus, as though it were being kneaded. Trussed and laid out raw with Craig standing next to my shoulder, not holding my hand, but peering over the lean-to that screened my belly, to see what I would never see of myself. Who imagines the exposures they'll come to when they clink their champagne glasses, dream crystally into the years? Craig's ash was coarse. Like grey sand mixed with dirt and irregular pebbles. Bone unbearably floated to mind. I rolled the grit between my fingers. Thought: this was the body I had lain beside for twenty-five years. Held that contradiction merely before it skittered off. But I had to keep something. Rubbed the matter that was Craig into the skin of my palms.

The package lay now in Zack's lap, as though undisturbed. It could only have been me who'd closed it back up.

* * *

"Mom?" Zack couldn't believe I was crying when it was such a sucky song. Why had he put it on the tape he'd made for the drive—Clapton's "You Look Wonderful Tonight"—not totally in his right mind, either. And here came my waterworks again. I had become a broken faucet. Flapping a hand to try to show I was all right, smiling zanily. Oh, great, he'd be in a state, now, worrying I was going to drive through tears and with a hand off the steering wheel while we were flying at a hundred and twenty clicks on a secondary highway.

"You know, Mom, this was your idea. No one says we have to go."

"He does. It's the only place for him. The book nook is, well, too confining. Perhaps that's idiotic. But."

"Daddy loved the water." We waited for Josh to say more. He'd said so little about his father, hardly mentioned his disappearance. What more was there?

Zack turned away from me, stared at nothing out the side window, but it was actually pretty at last, now that we'd passed the suburban barrens. The Credit River Valley opened on both sides of the road in rolling pasture.

"Daddy also liked to climb over rocks. Rocks and water and you couldn't get him back."

"Remember Vancouver Island with the tide coming in?" I prompted.

"He kept saying, 'Just a little farther . . .' And he kept turning up wet stones saying, 'Look, Pumpkin, another starfish.'"

There would never have been enough starfish to persuade Craig to turn around. Joshie's running shoes must have slipped and slid. The hood of his raincoat dripping onto his chin when he bent to see. His Daddy's glasses streaming like the rest of his face and the skin of Craig's K-way clinging drenched to his arm, melted to the flesh beneath.

"Have you been counting, Pumpkin? Sixteen? Let's see if we can find twenty."

From back behind the tide line, I tried to divine what they were up to. They were too far to hear me shouting them in, too near the water. Didn't Craig hear the surf getting louder? Joshie looking back to shore to try to spot me, a smudge of red anorak on the sand that he could see just because he knew I was there. If they left now, they'd be able to reach the packed sand where he could run if the sea came chasing them down. Craig loved the roar of it, the sea swelling his excitement, "Pumpkin, look at the colour of this one, have you ever seen so many!"

"Dad," Josh might yell over the waves, "I'm seven! I'm only seven!"

Craig would spin around to take in his boy, the unbelievable perspicacity of him. Too young to have seen much, or too young to drown? He was always humbled by the miracle that was his son, and would sober quickly at the hint that he was frightening him. "I'm coming, Pumpkin, don't worry."

"He turned his ankle," Josh later recounted. "He turned suddenly and slipped, came down hard on a knee. 'Christ the fucking knee,' Daddy said. 'What good's an athlete without a knee?' He didn't hear me crying, 'Daddy, your head.' I had to wipe his forehead and show him the red. He said, 'Go ahead, Pumpkin. Don't wait. I'll catch up. Go, Josh, you're fast.'"

* * *

Josh would have taken in the ocean, grey and heaving, the omnipresent wetness from above and below, all around. An obliterating vastness. How could his father love it so much as to risk all?

"Over there, Joshie," Craig had pointed when we'd come down to the water, "way over on the other side is Japan." In his mind's eye, Craig saw land, longed to dive in and swim across, felt no limits until shown proof—red.

Josh had to choose whether or not to set out alone on the slick, frothing rocks. Maybe he wanted to scream it again, but this time it came out like a plea: I'm only seven. He had to decide. His father might be a hero, but Josh was just a little boy. He scampered, forcing hands down when necessary for balance onto the inhospitable surfaces. Pushed ahead while always checking behind until I turned into a clear spot of colour, and he could run, the sand hard as a track. I'd been running too, because I met up with him breathless. "Stay!" a gasp as I punched towards the rocks.

Through tears in the car, I demanded, "What did he say exactly when he told you goodbye?"

Of course, Zack had gone over every word with me at the outset, more than once that first day, trying to grasp the incomprehensible.

I, too, had repeated it to those who arrived and called during the first week. How it conveyed so much, but ultimately nothing.

"Mom, do we have to do this? Do you have to make it harder?"

Josh in the back seat a palpable silence.

"We do, yes. We're going there to say goodbye. I want to know how he said it."

"But we've already told you a thousand times. Nothing's changed." Acerbically. "He hasn't exactly added anything."

"Daddy came downstairs to the basement," Josh piped, his tinkling kid's voice pitched higher than usual. Since the onset of Craig's last illness, Josh had made it his role to defuse confrontations. If Zack and I took chunks out of each other, who was going to be left?

"We were playing my new NBA 2000, me and Sammy and Tristan and Alex. Daddy said, 'Happy birthday, Pumpkin.' He kissed my head, said, 'I love you.' I said, 'Love you too, Dad.' Is that what he said to you, Zack?"

"Yeah, that's what he said." A growl.

"He didn't say goodbye?"

"No, Mom."

"He didn't say where he was going?"

"For Christ's sake, you know very well what happened. He said he was going for a walk. I was eating fucking birthday pancakes, and he came up from the basement and leaned over me like he was going to look at the box scores too. The fucking box scores, he had to have one last fucking look at them. He put his arms around my shoulders, kissed my head, too, and said that fucking 'I love you.' Yes, it did seem kind of weird, him getting all mushy just to go for a walk, but Dad was weird, right? So I didn't think twice about it."

Zack's voice had been rising, but now he shouted, "I fucking didn't think about it."

And through tears that he smacked with the heel of his hand. "Is that what you want to know?"

Sort of.

* * *

He'd broken from the leaves with a flash of red wings and an insistent cry: "I'm not mad." As in lucid. And perhaps, I hoped, "I'm not mad," as in angry. Not angry, a fluttering absolution.

I'd recognized the anger when the policeman told me. Paused time and again between the calls and the kids and the house filling with care: he was so mad at me, so damn mad. Not to say a word, leave a word, no goodbye, forget the I love you after a quarter century of two lives so intertwined a tweaked thread could unmake the whole.

I had fled the house, leaving his head bent low over a plate of pancakes. So relieved to escape for an hour. Because he was home again. I'd brought him back from hospital just the previous morning, thinking now what? A man on permanent disability, not yet forty-four years old. A man with a premature shuffle, that milky film over the eyes, the slack jawed gape at Zack's school basketball games, and worst of all his needing to be led, compliantly waiting for the tug at his collar. Not who I married. Those were good days when I didn't call 911 because he couldn't breathe, he was screaming, thudding against the wall, the children terrified in the doorway. Or when I had to herd him into the car to head off the point of crisis, talking him down through the interminable minutes to the hospital as he threatened to throw himself out. Pounding at the car window and I awash in adrenalin sweat. Talking myself as much as him through it.

How much do people have to talk themselves through a marriage?

He took me to the beach for the first time on our honeymoon, called me his Jewish Venus, black swimsuit, gold in my ears and looped around my neck, the new gold rings awkward on our fingers. Swung me over his shoulder, carried me not over a threshold but into a blinding glare of mirrored sun and the bite of Great Lake water. I wrapped my legs around his waist, pressed the water from between our chests seeking warmth, but it flooded back in, a northerly temperature in June. He bore me away from shore in long strides along the sandy bottom until we were just two heads bobbing a kilometre out and I'd have had to swim if he let me go.

Cold pockets that made my flesh rise even once we were accustomed to it. The cool tenderness between us became our element. Only now did I see how far we'd drifted beyond our depth.

I brought Craig home, my once-handsome, driven-to-achieve husband, the incisive intelligence dulled, scathing humour buried inside a fearful husk. His real self shrivelled and rattling within. Tagging along a step or two outside our circle at the children's theatre, at the soccer games; a silent, oppressive presence at the head of the table.

I called out in relief, so happy to abscond for an hour or so. Hanging up my apron, my last glimpse of him a head bent low over the plate of pancakes. So eager to get out for the blessed hour it took to get my hair cut. They pretended, the doctors and the specialists, that he was discharged into my care, but I couldn't be with him every minute, it was a fact. So I left, calling out from the front door, "See you later."

Could you believe the glib farewell? I was sick over it. In my haste to be off, out, clear of him. Waiting upstairs on the bed all the long morning, building his resolve while the house filled with the smell of frying batter. Staying upstairs so as not to cast a pall over the children's breakfast, to let Joshie enjoy his last sweet pleasure of birthday delight. Self-abnegating as always, he came down for the leftovers. I hung my apron on the magnetized hook on the refrigerator, glanced at the top of his thick-haired head, heard a low, "Mm, this is so good."

There it was. Food and children, home and hearth, the heavy, delicious taste of air. What he had to give up so that life would go on as it should, as it had before the disruption that had no place in our child-protecting household. He had known what to do. He was a dad, a man who loved his family more than life itself. There in the, "Mm, this is so-o-o good," was his intent.

* * *

Six in the morning, and the beach was empty, not even a single, early dog walker. A sun-white overlay had already washed some blue from the sky, spilling it into the lake that surged to greet us. Joshie kicked off his flip-flops and rushed in up to his knees before he ran back shouting.

"Crazy cold," he yelled, while I tried to clasp him to my side to both warm him and calm him down. It was our opportunity. I'd put it off; by tomorrow there'd be guests. This had to be the day, and the weather mercifully wasn't gloomy. We had come early enough to have the beach to ourselves. If the water was cold, well, it wasn't meant to be easy.

"Shh, Honey. We'd like to have the beach to ourselves for a bit. How come it's so cold though, when all summer it's been hot as Hades?"

"Undertow," said Zack. "Must have brought it in overnight from way out deep."

"Don't worry, Baby. You don't have to come in with us. Zack and I will take the bag of ashes out to the third sandbar. We'll save some and come back for you."

I'd said it, there, the word 'ashes,' not just 'sprinkling.'

If it were midday and I was braving this water, there'd have been whoops and shrieks of "You've got to be kidding!" with Zack taunting, "squawk, squawk," chicken style. Instead, sharp, silent intakes with each inch deeper. Zack a couple of feet ahead holding the bag. There'd be the stretch between the second and third sandbars he'd have to breast through with one arm. I turned back to wave to Joshua, a small dancing figure on the shoreline framed by dunes and further on the scrubby cedars that formed a second horizontal beneath the white-gold eastern sky.

The lake was warmer on the third sandbar when I splashed up to find Zack peering inside, expecting Craig maybe to waft from between the folds of wrinkled plastic. I dipped my hand into the bag for a fistful, moved to toss the ashes overhand, send Craig flying in an arc, but Zack stayed my hand. "Don't be nuts, Mom. The wind's blowing in."

So we took turns, yes, sprinkling him. The ash spread briefly coating the water. We watched it float and sink, another kind of sand that would blend in with the rest. I thought, perhaps we'd pick up grains of it on our towels on future vacations, or in our hair and the creases of our clothes. Ending up in the corners of the battered beach suitcase I'd never again vacuum clean.

Zack pushed to shore to pick up his brother. I followed slowly. What to do now with the plastic bag and twist tie and box, cardboard, and brown paper, nothing but wrapping like the shirts and ties and jackets that would hold his form for only so long?

I waited at the first sandbar, while Zack carried Joshie towards me high in his arms, the child's long Craig-like feet skimming the cool surface. The day's wind had started up, stirring the cedars in the distance and raising the flesh on shoulders and arms. Josh shifted his white tennis hat to my head. I poured the last grains from the bag into his palm. He regarded them, then closed his fist, and plunged it in. Underwater, the child's thumb opened first and then one slow finger at a time.

This was who we were now, mother and sons. Zack unbolted his clasp, releasing his brother through the chute of his arms. Josh splashed about for warmth. "Come on, Freak-face, I'll race you in." My eldest held back to let his brother get the jump on him, but Josh, disoriented, said, "Don't feel like it."

What we felt was absence. Craig gone. Yet how much more so once we turned our backs and left his dust behind to the storms that would crash over him, pummelling and pounding and casting him ever farther? We braced ourselves in the chill sway as the needle swung wildly, true north untethered and lost. Ahead, the sun white as a mirror had erased the horizon. Behind, water fused with sky. The lake slapped and pressed at our backs as we squinted, trying to make out the mirage-like shimmer of shore.

A Human Condition

N O LAUGHING MATTER, yet it warmed me to think of us locked in a *folie à deux*, two bright women (the diplomas on the wall attested to the accomplishment of my therapist, at least) sitting opposite each other, so close their knees almost touched. The doctor had her right hand raised with a finger in the air. The raised arm had been wagging for so long it called for reinforcement. She was supporting it at the elbow with her other hand. We made a comic picture, and one had to find the laughs where one could.

Ignoring my wisecrack, she shuffled her chair even closer. She had a sense of humour but opted to sober me up. Follow her finger with my eyes only, she directed. Neither of us was oblivious to the flim-flammery feel of it. "Promise not to report me to the psychoanalytic institute," she'd quipped before we'd started. I was scared, but had refused the anti-depressants the MD in her initially proposed. I'd watched my late husband lose his mind, first on his own steam and then driven further to distraction by the variety of mood-altering drugs thrown at his illness. I would not cross that threshold, nor could I rely forever on the bitter blue sleeping pills, the godsend that was the only thing that shut my eyes and allowed me a night's rest. It wasn't that I tossed and turned and felt lumps in the mattress. It was more like my eyes had dried up after hours in a sauna and were now stuck open in perpetuity, my gateway to consciousness thrown wide to interlopers all and sinisterly sundry. The longer I stayed awake, the more impossible it seemed that they would ever again lower their lids to release me. In fact, I could barely blink. I remembered once saying to Craig when he too had not been able to sleep, his breath short, voice pitched to squeaking, "No one ever died of missing a night's sleep." What a sorry attempt at consolation. The toxic zinging under my skin must have had something to do with my racing pulse. This was my punishment for surviving Craig, for surviving Craig's illness, and for having the gall to try to live again: my children's remaining parent next in line to lose her mind.

My therapist had assured me this wasn't the case, but rather a consequence and delayed reaction to years of assaults on my nervous system. It was part of a condition in the DSM (*Diagnostic and Statistical Manual of Mental Disorders*) called PTSD (post-traumatic stress disorder). An SSRI (selective serotonin re-uptake inhibitor) is typically prescribed. My family doctor's more prosaic solution to the narrower problem of sleep was these notched blue pills, which she encouraged me to break in half along the notch if I thought I might need them for a prolonged period.

How long did it take to get over twenty-five years of living, not on the edge of disaster—more like the cusp of foreboding? Disaster *might* have struck at any moment. My late, high-achieving husband might have quit his job out of a sense of failure and self-disgust, even if he'd just received a merit-based bonus, or he might have threatened to, rebounding the following day, charged up by a new idea. During his final illness, I'd carried a phone in my pocket at all times to be able to call for help—not only for him but also for me and the kids if he was bedevilled enough to turn against us.

I generally valued my family practitioner's low-interventionist approach, but at this juncture, it felt niggardly of her to offer only time-limited relief. The bottle contained dispiritingly few blue pills. "They are addictive, you know," she chided, not without sympathy, but firmly no less.

"Describe the upsetting experience again, while following my finger with your eyes."

Her hand was small and rounded, like the rest of her. Unlike mine, which showed its love of soil and disdain of gloves, the skin of her forefinger was smooth and pale, the nail neatly curved. It oscillated evenly, an irritating distraction eating up my precious fifty minutes.

"When I think of that moment, getting up from the table. The sun was overhead, blinding, and it was hot. Like getting up too quickly, you know, and you kind of white out. Like that. Such a beautiful day. So bright, warm. Summer. Summer for me, you know, but nothing anymore for him. Nowhere for him. Yet me, free, warm, given my life back."

I was weeping through this, snatching at tissues that weren't up to the job. "Everything ahead of me. It felt annihilating. The glaring white emptiness of the future. That's how all of this started, with the woman at the fair. What she said made my heart swallow itself whole. Out of seven on the badness scale, how does it feel? A five at least, not that I mean it's like the worst that has happened, but pretty close to how bad I can feel if you count that as being as real on some level as what takes place in fact. On a scale of the subjective reality, I'd say about a five point six six six, etc., out of seven."

My doctor didn't flicker even the faintest of smiles. "A five and two-thirds on the discomfort scale in the area of your heart, is that right?"

I nodded. I aimed to be a good patient and chose this doctor because she seemed pre-eminently adult. We were adults here. My problem from the outset, over a year ago, could not have been more grim. She had stressed, engaging me eye-to-eye: "I know about chronic illness." Yet it was now that the crisis was over that I was forced to see her not twice, but sometimes three times weekly, stumbling from one session to the next.

"Let's go back to that scene." Her voice didn't break the silence so much as land like a leaf on water. "It's a beautiful summer's day. You feel the warmth and light on your skin, in your eyes. You're at a local fair with your son. The whole world seems new to you, bright and beckoning. How do you feel walking into that scene?"

"Lucky. Almost unbearably so. Such a luxury to be able to drop in like that instead of rushing home in case, you know, or dreading a visit to hospital. Not having to go to the hospital that day, to be free of it forever. Of sitting across from him in a booth in the cafeteria. If we chanced to get a booth and didn't have to share a table. Sharing a table, you know what that was like? While he slumped, eyes beseeching mine for hours, repeating, 'Chief, I'm so scared. I'm so scared,' day in and day out for months. Not able to do more than sit with him and listen while staffers in their scrubs munched away beside us without missing a beat, then gathered up their garbage, returned to their work. We sat, suffering on through all the consecutive diners happy to claim the vacated seats. It seems unreal but also too real, a heightened real. I'm hyper aware of being free to step into a normal scene and not feel set apart from it."

"Go into your body. When you think of that excitement, where in your body does it resonate?"

This time I didn't have to guess. "In my chest. Like a first day of school flutter, but without anxiety."

"Are you sure, about the anxiety I mean?"

"Expectant, on the lip of the springboard."

"On a scale of one to seven, how troubling is that prospect?"

The finger hadn't wavered. My eyes had fallen in with its rhythm.

"Zero. It belongs on a different scale. Six or seven on the pleasure meter."

"So you're happy, and free. And Josh?"

"He's okay, maybe not thrilled but not averse to going along with it for a while."

"So nothing is making you uncomfortable."

"It feels like heaven even though the fair is just peanuts, a backyard gathering of locals, and a few passersby like us. Home-baked goodies, candy apples, games for little kids. Not much of interest for Josh. We took in the information booth about the history of the cottage and the challenge to save it. No reason really to hang around once we'd browsed through the pamphlets and made a donation. But I didn't want to leave. We must have arrived early because the woman was just setting up her table. She had her back to me. I saw her tie the flowery scarf behind her ears. 'Look, Josh, a fortune teller!' I couldn't resist, though I know from experience how suggestible I am. Whatever's said stays with me for years; it's stupid. I said, 'Josh, why don't you buy us some treats while I have my fortune read.'"

My eyes filmed, making it harder to track the finger.

"On a scale of one to seven, how uncomfortable do you feel at this moment?"

"For crying out loud! Does it have to matter? Okay, maybe a four or a three, who the heck knows? An f-ing five then! It was a mistake. I should have hightailed it out of there at the sight of the scarf. Do you believe it? A two-dollar fortune teller at a backyard fair to save Alexander Muir's cottage. The composer of 'The Maple Leaf Forever.' It was all so innocent. We were on the porch saying goodbye after Joshua's piano lesson, when his teacher happened to mention, 'Oh, there's the fair a couple of blocks away. Joshua, remember that tune you played last year?' She sang the opening bars in her operatic voice. Right there outside on the porch, so lovely. 'Alexander Muir wrote it in this neighbourhood, and the very tree is in front of the cottage. Wish I could go too, but Saturday's booked with you students.'" And I thought, why not? Such a lovely melody, way nicer than 'O Canada.'

Way nicer than 'O Canada' would you believe? Nicer than 'O Canada' is what took me to find out a fortune teller could not see my future. She turned up the cards and saw nothing there. Like the one time I read the *I Ching* with a friend, me nineteen and she a year younger. She threw the die, and we turned to the passage. "What does that mean?" she asked, and I shrugged. But the passage read that there was no future. Within three years she was dead, killed by a hit and run she obviously hadn't seen coming! Can you believe that in my new-found freedom I brought this fresh doom on myself? If my future isn't discernible, it's no great leap to guess why I'm loathe to close my eyes. For twenty-five years I refused to see the signs that Craig wasn't neurotic in a conventional sense, that there was something gravely wrong with him. Did I need any further convincing to keep my eyes peeled on what might come around the corner?

* * *

If one maintained an ironic remove, stepped outside the panic to laugh, however ruefully, all couldn't be lost. I held on to this caveat as my therapist led me through the steps of this new method of assuaging post-traumatic stress. She was in the process of attending training workshops in EMDR—eye movement desensitization reprocessing, a real clunker of a name.

After each workshop, we revised our approach. For a few sessions, my eyes followed the metronomic waggle of her finger while she guided me down the wormhole of whatever disturbing image had come to mind. We had established a 'safe place' in my imagination to which I resorted after each plunge into the underbrush. We assessed my difficulty with the central image on a scale of one to seven, and rated the complications this image or memory caused in my current life. Next, I had to identify the area in my body that this image affected, where I felt it and how it felt, and the discomfort of the sensation on the wearisome scale.

The finger business was cumbersome. A few workshops in, she learned that the actual movement of the eyes was not central after all, and that it was more likely the bilateral stimulation of both hemispheres of the brain that helped to open up the boundaries between them, releasing memories and constructive associations. Now she had me tapping my shoulders alternately with arms crossed over my chest, hardly less ridiculous, but at least not as tiring for her. As she pulled her chair into my personal space, I realized I would have missed it if she hadn't. I felt supported in almost a physical sense by her proximity. At the end of the exercise, I returned to the 'safe place,' and then used the same scale to enumerate my responses in each of the categories, noting if there was any change.

Analytical and individualistic all my days, one might have expected me to spurn this cookie-cutter approach to mining the recesses of my precious, idiosyncratic subconscious. Sarcastic and leery at the start of each session, I was yet eager to engage. Craig's illness and death had cut me down to size. Contrary to my expectations, my love and steadfastness had not ultimately stemmed the tide of his undoing. Still, I had to try to save myself. In my humbled state, I was ready to accept that I wasn't too special to benefit from a one-size-fits-all approach.

I was supposed to use aspects of it when anxiety overtook me during the day. Mentally take cover in my safe place. Failing that, cross my arms and start tapping while I identified what was troubling me, where it manifested in my body, run the numbers, work my way through it. However valid or not the theory behind the practice, I agreed with my doctor that it gave me something concrete to fall back on to bring my symptoms and maybe even my brain chemistry into line. The sleeplessness had been just the start it seemed, and while still the primary presenting symptom, its attendant minions had set up camp in my waking mind.

Friends and loved ones did their best to help. My adult niece and her friend took me to the cinema to see a comedy. But no sooner than we were seated, the images in the trailer seemed to break into frenetically pulsing pinpoints of light that took me to the extremity of vibrating colour. Everything beat too fast, too bright, too loud. I flashed my niece a wild smile: "Freak out, I'm afraid." The house lights weren't dim enough to let me start my embarrassing shoulder tapping. Everyone was already seated when I gathered my things, started with the 'excuse me's' as I bumped by knees, and stepped on feet on my way to the aisle. At the back of the theatre, I settled down to tapping. I pictured my doctor's full face under her short, gamin-style hair. She gave me a nod, while I prayed that when the movie started, the images wouldn't be as hectic or the sound a roar. The comedy opened with a scene in which the main character had to hide during a home invasion, and witness her boyfriend getting scalped. What was really funny, though, was that she ended up with PTSD. Well, it *was*. One had to be able to step outside the frame to maintain the ironic remove. Even as one madly drummed one's shoulders. "Eet eez ze life," a friend from Paris had inimitably stated. If I stopped being able to laugh at myself, I'd know I was in serious trouble.

* * *

I couldn't wait to tell my therapist about the movie, about finding myself within a scene so tailored to my black humour. I jumped right in before we'd even set up our chairs, and as though I'd held a carrot in front of her nose, the Socratic guide in her took the bait.

"When you imagine not laughing at your pain, what do you feel?"

"Embarrassed, like having no clothes on in public. My sister could have pierced my eardrum when I told her on the phone that Craig was dead. And Craig, even when he wasn't talking about his suffering, when he was describing his work, for instance, it was always 'major this, and major that' in high seriousness with no sense of perspective. You'd think he'd split the atom."

"You feel it's inappropriate to take oneself seriously?"

"Too seriously. There is always room for higher achievement, deeper catastrophe, greater injustice, further deprivation, etc."

"When you think of the worst that could happen, what image comes to mind?"

The level of discomfort in my chest, in my throat, in my stuffed nostrils was seven. I was literally choking. I saw my six-year-old half-sister, dead ten years before I was born. She was a skinny, naked child in a gas chamber of naked people. Her naked mother's soft body and strong arms enveloped her but could not protect her as the Zyklon B gas descended from the ceiling, taking the tallest first.

"Her mother's name was Mancika. She was short, like you." I stared pointedly at my doctor. "She would have seen it coming." There was no finger wagging going on. No shoulder tapping. We had stumbled straight to the chase, unarmed. "The children were last to die, so my half-sister might have had just enough time to feel her mother's arms fall away."

* * *

Because Craig had died in the spring, our kids had been exempted from finishing the school year. Before school started again, I bought a new pair of glasses to replace the old wire-rimmed ovals. These were black plastic. They drew attention to my face. There was something challenging about the new glasses. 'Widow' was an awful word. It evoked veils and retirement from the world. Weeds. Widow's weeds, perforce strangulating. "In your face!" I said to that.

Before his father died, my youngest had been tested for an enriched program. It had required him to move to a new school where we knew no one. This school was much larger than the other, more ethnically and demographically diverse. He hadn't objected to the switch. No one knew us there. No one was aware of our recent loss. He didn't have to be the boy whose dad had just died, although we arrived doubly estranged to the schoolyard carrying our singularity like something outside ourselves, a bulky box that had to be put aside whenever we started a conversation with a stranger. I tried not to transfer my inner immigrant-child's fear of being different and not knowing the ropes. I showed my son how to claim his place by chatting up whichever mom happened to take a seat beside me on the cement tree planter as we awaited the morning bell. I was the new mother in the trendy glasses with the beautiful boy who leaned against her legs wearing his newness bravely, biding his time. I looked around the schoolyard Craig had never stepped foot in, to the playing field that hadn't heard his voice cheering our son on, and my head swooned, yanked from one dimension to another. I watched my baby line up with his class outside the steel double doors that opened to swallow the knapsacked little internees into the dark brick edifice. I nodded to him as he turned, smiled, and showed him what I had never felt, that it was safe to step into the unknown.

You'd walked a long way down the road aware of a weight dragging at your ankles, and you'd given it a name, let's say 'Craig'. Craig, his tall, large-boned but lanky frame. In his youth, the long, thick, straight hair had poured down his back. His thin face with its square chin. The full, undefined lips, well-formed nose, downturned eyes as though nature had anticipated the depths of his travail. All the while, behind his tall frame and its long shadow, a small, skinny girl had stood naked and obscured.

How much of me was her—how much of my life I may have forfeited—
I wasn't sure I should see.

It's been eighteen years since Craig took his life; fifteen since my
therapist's chronic illness had returned with a vengeance, ripping her
away. Despite our vigilance to stay sharp and on the lookout, the future's
favourite trick is to blindside us. It took my good doctor, but gave me
someone else, the mate of my latter years. I thought of rocks speeding
through space. They were chaos, unfated, random, unlike the moons
revolving around their planets, the planets around their suns, and the
stars spiralling in their galaxies, suggesting a kind of narrative. John tried
to explain their natural order to me, but what I saw was the great blind
eye of the universe receding as it expanded, while we, not even motes of
consciousness, flickered in and out interchangeably. On a human scale
of one to seven, this boundless indifference barely moved the needle.

Red

EVERYDAY I TOOK A walk in the leafy neighbourhood south of the new development where John and I had moved. On our new streets, the trees were no higher than the three-storey roofs. The cardinals had not yet crossed Gerrard Street to nest in our leggy oaks, preferring the century-old foliage south of the divide between then and now. Cardinals rarely left Southern Ontario, although I didn't often hear or see them on my winter walks. Come spring, they called from the topmost bare branches. This day in July, one posed against a clear sky from a rooftop aerial. Just the lines of the aerial against a cloudless blue, with the red silhouette tracking his mate. I thought of it as Craig, just as I had recognized him at dawn the day following his death, a red streak from the garden of our old house to the uppermost leaves one fence over. Whenever he called to me on my walks, I stopped to spot him, listened a few moments, and then charged him with the task of looking out for our sons. I had a right to his help. All single parents wish for input from someone who cares as much about their kids as they do.

I went on an Alaskan cruise with my mother and my sister a year after Craig died. It wasn't for my sake, but for my mother's. In her early eighties, she wasn't up to travelling on her own. Not since my sister's marriage at the age of twenty had we three been together for as long as a week, let alone bunked in a single stateroom.

My sister is a tiny woman. I, like my mother once, have been forced to accept voluptuousness. After Craig took his life, I gained. I still worked out at the gym and followed my usual routines, but it was as if, having been reduced to half of the couple we'd been, I'd added girth to replace the missing limb.

Around that time, my therapist began her dying. I hadn't been aware that shortly before we'd started our work together, she had suffered from cancer. She was my mainstay through the last, worst year of Craig's illness. Then her cancer returned, this time resisting treatment. She wondered if I was putting on weight to compensate for her waning. These were sessions filled with tears. I had been crying since Craig died. Now I was crying for her. It's hard to imagine the dedication and courage it must have taken to spend the last year of her able life, her life in the world, listening to an assortment of clients snivelling over her imminent end. Despite my regard for her opinion, I didn't agree. Craig and I together had been one; now I was reduced by half. Despite the fact that we didn't fit together (not like two jigsaw puzzle pieces that mesh, but rather two pieces that almost mesh, so that you think they might even if you know they won't), on some level, I still aspired to the whole.

Shipboard, my mother played bridge, while my sister read on a lounger in the shade. I ran my laps on the track around the pool deck. Playing my role as the youngest, I offered to take a top bunk so they might have the two lower berths. We shared the tiny bathroom peaceably. In fact, after my noisy childhood, during which at least two of us had usually been locked in verbal combat, it was surprising that no altercation disrupted the voyage. Perhaps we were mindful of each other's diminishments: my mother's advanced years, my bereavement, my sister's menopausal fretting over where she'd misplaced her sunglasses or ship card.

A year earlier, after Craig's memorial, once everyone had gone back to their lives and my sister again was a voice on the line from the city where we'd been raised, she gave me this advice: accept all invitations. She spoke from experience learned from divorce. I tried, once spring turned to summer. I carted my youngest son with me from one friend's cottage to another, smiling, swimming, and sipping gin and tonic. I hadn't put on weight yet. I bought two new bathing suits and felt good in them. Then one night, my eyes refused to close. There would be no shortcut. I had to study my way into widowhood: going to the movies alone on Saturday nights, taking long walks by myself, and eating out with my book for company. There was no reason it should come naturally after twenty-five years as half of a couple. I had to force my nose into it, acknowledge—no, learn what wasn't there. Fill in for it, fill up with something else. Fill out.

The ship made various ports of call. My mother disembarked occasionally, once to shop for gemstones for her daughters and granddaughters. Another day, we took a narrow-gauge railway ride on the Alaskan side of the Yukon Trail corridor. She seemed happy to stay on board with her bridge buddies and not miss her afternoon nap so she might be fresh for the evening song and dance revue, her favourite part of each day. My sister and I were free to take hikes together and to visit the museums.

I got it into my head to go on a helicopter ride up to the Mendenhall Glacier, although I had never liked heights. During childhood, I dreamt of hanging off one end of Montreal's Jacques Cartier Bridge as it lifted. The roadway tipped down, spilling the car carrying my family towards the other shore, while I clung, rising ever higher over the broad St. Lawrence. On gondolas, sweat dripped from my palms as I clutched the support posts. I played miniature golf in amusement parks, while others went on the rides.

I couldn't explain why a person with a crippling fear as mine would insist on not missing out on this expedition. I thought of how my boys would have enjoyed it, but then again, had the boys been with me, the expense for the three of us would have proved prohibitive. I reasoned that going solo was a great savings, a bargain, and thus not to be passed up. My sister abstained for her own good reasons.

A shiny red helicopter, gently rocking heel to toe and then tilting its nose up so as to taste the brilliant northern air before lifting off, is a work of art in motion. I felt privileged to watch each make its ascent. I didn't doubt my decision for a moment, single though I was, the only single person in line, with no one to hold my sweaty hand when, inevitably, I would feel sure to slip and plummet to my death. Our pilot promised us that he was of age to drive a car. He looked twelve. The other four passengers were all in their twenties. There I was alone, the widow, my youth gone with the remains burned in a box. The things you hold in your head when you're on the brink. A woman on a cruise. The ashes of her husband that she'd rolled in her palms.

I'm superstitious, but my left brain laughs it off. It is only now, these many years later, that I recognize the cardinals I addressed on my daily walks in the red helicopter as it had swung out its tail to present its cheek to the bluest of skies. Perhaps that was why I heard its engine's call. Its redness, its resting bird shape, the blue of the Alaskan sky. Craig took me on that flight.

The pilot's voice in the headphones was eager to show us. Did we realize how lucky we were? All summer long, the range had been shrouded in fog. Fog here crashed like a curtain on a bad act. Except these acts were stupendous. I had seen it for myself the day before, as we'd edged out of Juneau's harbour. The town hugged the waterside. Eagles, unaffected by the scale and surge of our ship, or the looming, white-capped grandeur behind them, held their posts along the quay like guiding totems. From one moment to the next, a curtain dropped on the left side of the scene, wiping out eagles, posts, and pier; on the right, the mountains and the town continued to flash in the late afternoon sun. The pilot said he'd been flying tourists all summer but had been able to show them only the most immediate mountains en route to the Mendenhall. Today—his excited voice was as unfiltered as a child's—the whole range was visible. If we didn't mind losing some minutes of our time on the glacier, he'd take us around a few extra peaks.

Didn't mind! Take us around! In quest of replicating the thrill, I would later persuade my future husband to fly with me in a chopper over the Grand Canyon and over the limestone formations off the southern coast of Australia. Recently we'd hovered over a mesa-like formation rising out of a Norwegian fjord. Although these flights were each a pleasure, none of them proved to be the revelation this first one was as our young pilot clung to each rock face, hugging the banks and ridges of the Coast Range. We swept up one side and down the other, aswoon with rock and air. Who said there wasn't a God? That the heavens hadn't opened up for just my moment of deliverance? I did, but it hardly mattered if one made use the trope to take the leap.

At that height, our conveyance as slight as a bird next to the great monuments of nature, I let go the tether that had bound me to grief.

Sitting Shiva

AT FIFTY YEARS OF AGE, one might say I was lucky to have had only four funerals under my belt. My father's funeral fourteen years earlier had been the first. Jewish funeral rites and protocol had still been news to me. I was the only one of my father's style-conscious women to show up in makeup, leather boots, and an Italian knit. Who knew that as a principal mourner I was expected to rend my blouse and appear unadorned, almost penitent before the fact of mortality? My sister and I had been spared childhood funerals by the crematoria of the Nazis. After I fled Montreal for graduate school, my sister and mother joined two separate congregations, both more traditional than the Reformed synagogue of my youth. While I continued as non-practising, they turned to observant circles that put them in the know. I stared aghast at my mother in a worn black pullover and around-the-house pants. More confusing was how a dun-coloured rag shredded at the collar had found its way into my sister's discriminating wardrobe.

Most of Montreal's Jews are buried by Paperman & Sons. In 1990, when my father died, Paperman's, as it's cozily known, was still at the more upscale address on Côte-des-Neiges, not far north of the cemetery on Mount Royal where the city's earlier personages of means had booked the best berths for eternity. Urban land has grown too costly, even for the reasonably well-off dead. My father's funeral procession headed north and east to Duvernay, a suburb that seems to have flourished on interment. By the time my mother's third and final husband, Max, died not long before the new millennium, Paperman's had also moved north in response to the direction of their trade, into more sprawling premises among the banquet halls and kitchen and bath emporia along Rue Jean Talon.

Craig's didn't count as a funeral. Craig belonged to me and our boys, memorialized our own way without funeral home, denominational service, or public venue. He had been a private man who had suffered an isolating disease of the mind. Outside his family, his work had meant everything to him, but no one he had worked alongside, leading, mentoring, and protecting them from the exactions of corporate greed, had approached him in the eighteen months of his terminal bout of clinical depression. He had given himself to his work, inspiring both respect and affection. Yet not a single colleague or member of his staff had called or come to visit. I got it, to a point. People don't know how to react when someone they've come to know in a certain way turns out to be—or to also be—someone else. A man always circumspect about his personal life, perhaps they felt they were honouring his privacy. I had watched him suffer alone, so I did not feel charitable in the wake of his suicide. I insisted on a private memorial in his own home among his loved ones and our closest friends. With my door closed against those who had abandoned him, his former colleagues held their own memorial at his workplace.

They used the word 'closure' in the lingua franca of business. They asked a minister to speak, never mind that Craig had abhorred religion from his earliest days in Sunday school. Having been invited to attend, I sat in the front row, our two sons on either side of me. I wore a black dress purchased for one of his office's interminable Christmas banquets, where we'd been expected to sit at the executives' table while yearning for refuge among Craig's staff, thinking darkly that it must have been intended all along for this, my late husband's misconceived commemoration.

For all my harsh thoughts, I had agreed to participate. To give Craig his due, I spoke. I had lain in the bath the previous day, mentally assembling his monument. Neither before nor since have I spoken publicly without relying on a written script. The best speech I ever gave and not a word remembered. It was easy. Everything was easy by comparison to telling each child, first one, and then the other, that their father had killed himself.

I was now on my way to my first Jewish memorial service in Toronto, wearing the same black dress, which had apparently become my funeral costume. I pretty much swam in it now. I had lost the weight I'd gained after Craig died, and then some. My life had changed course. I belong to the straddle generation of second-wave feminists for whom a new man in her life might still change its trajectory. I drove across the city alone and found Benjamin's Park Memorial Chapel to be almost identical to its counterpart in Montreal, as at home on the broad commercial stretch of Steeles Avenue as Paperman's on its Jean Talon digs. In the parking lot, I worked on getting myself out of the car. I sat sideways in the seat, staring at my legs extended on the asphalt. I don't wear pantyhose as a rule, so my legs appeared disembodied in the black nylon.

* * *

I swore I wasn't going to let myself be swept up in the sadness of this funeral. I felt bound to this. Because I loved her in a direct, uncomplicated way, as one can love only someone at the periphery of one's life. Someone gazing quietly and empathically through a one-way mirror. She did me only good. Do not grieve, she might have said, for the good work we did together. She called it our work—not my problem, but ours to puzzle through together. A professional commonplace no doubt but effective just the same if the patient's convinced. I felt grateful to see myself as her patient, not a client in a mercantile relationship, but a patient in receipt of care. She was the bank beside the rapids sweeping my family to the brink. Once a week, I got to climb out to catch my breath. I can't adequately convey the relief I felt to be momentarily on the receiving end when I was the sole caregiver of my children and my husband was seriously ill.

How could it be, I had asked myself after our first session, that this rare find had an opening in her schedule? It's not easy for a discerning shopper to dig up a good therapist. I had started with a list of referrals. Each doctor, their practice full, suggested another set of names. I worked my way through them systematically, and sat for four interviews with those who had available time slots. It made an amusing story when I described these sessions to friends, the unsuitability, to put it mildly, of the practitioners with time on their hands. But therapy isn't a dinner party.

Her name was at the bottom of my third tier of candidates. I wasn't hopeful as I entered the side door of an oversized cement block in an unduly prosperous neighbourhood. It was early in the day, but my nose picked up the scent of stewing brisket. Friday, I registered, *erev sabat*. The stairs led up to a closed door but also hooked downwards. Kitchen, I thought, sniffing up, so I descended. The house's footprint was Yeti-sized. A long hallway, not particularly well-lit, with a glass-walled empty waiting room to the side. In search of the washroom, I passed a closed door from behind which came a murmur. The hall continued until I found what I wanted, but I had a sense of other chambers dark and sepulchral. Nothing in the environs suggested warmth and approachability, both on my must-have list. At a certain age, one derives no small pleasure in having one's expectations upended. Within the buried recesses of her house, I found a gem of a quiet individual.

Listening to the eulogists from one of the back pews in Benjamin's, I wondered if her nearest and dearest would laugh to hear her described as quiet. I sat alone and grieved alone among a congregation of around two hundred mourners. It felt right to think of it as a congregation. The eulogists all mentioned the synagogue community she'd been a founding member of and continued to lead. Being Jewish, they each maintained, was the cornerstone of her life. One described the authority of her voice.

She never led me. I'm not sure she always guided. She cleared a space for my mutterings, otherwise drowned out by Craig's desperation and dread. One of the first things she said after I described my situation had been, "I know from chronic illness." I noted the preposition 'from' and its assumption of a shared heritage. I called her on it. She wondered why I positioned myself outside the Jewish community. Did she really think this was the road to head down first, I rebuked, when I had a husband who was losing his mind? She excused herself. But I assumed she expected that in due course, our primary concern confronted, we'd tackle the dissonant chord she heard in my composition. On this, we differed from beginning to end.

The beginning, like a snake, tail in its teeth, suggested our end. I had heard 'from' rather than 'chronic illness.' I never associated 'chronic illness' with her name at the bottom of the referrals. I hadn't questioned my luck. "It was so worth it, brief as the time for our work was. For real. I mean it." She didn't lose her composure when I made these declarations. Only I succumbed to tears. Even when she first told me she was dying. There I was going on about whatever. Something, how she held her hands in her lap as though she were holding her own hand, made me stop. "Is anything the matter?" She looked taken aback, then drew a breath. "Unfortunately, I'm afraid so." She told me there was no hope. She and her husband had sat seized up and uncomprehending in the specialist's office. She had recovered from the illness a little more than three years back and had been given the green light to resume her life and her practice. That was then. She lowered her head a little. I sniffed and babbled. "It was so worth it, what you did for me and all your other clients during these last three years. The work of therapy like what we aim to do in life is never really finished anyway."

Okay, so I didn't say that last bit, but presumably at some point during the months of sobbing to come—months that could not have been more crushingly tagged in therapy-speak as 'terminating'—I must have, given the solipsistic nature of the exercise, let slip something just as awful. All of us grieving patients likely dropped the wrong line at least once from our blubbering broken hearts.

She'd stood up to say goodbye at our last appointment. "It's been an honour to know you," she said, staring steadily into my eyes. If these were her words to each of us, they still felt selected for me. She was always small and a bit roundish. The illness had taken its pounds of flesh. I couldn't say what the absence of those pounds felt like when I gathered her in my arms, except that they were more palpable than the bones that still held her upright.

I had written her biweekly letters since we'd parted a year earlier. She didn't answer my letters, nor did I expect her to. In them, I assured her as much. But I did hope that while she was still able to pick up her own mail, she would read them. Even of that I could not be certain. How could I know where her professional life divided from her personal arena? She had given her patients all that she could while she still had the strength, without wavering in her diligence. But once she closed the door to her basement office and ascended the stairs for the last time into her private quarters, did she also close the door completely on the part of herself that had flourished there?

Anything I'd know about the particulars of her life, I found out at her funeral. A friend spoke, and her sister spoke about their lives as children, their family of origin, and the Jewish youth camps they'd attended and later became counsellors at. How she'd forged a leadership role for women within the ancient practices she treasured. A colleague limned her professional activities. A few words from her son were subsumed by emotion. The theme of Jewishness ran through it all. It brought back the smell of brisket from my Friday morning sessions and that very first interview when I told her to shelve the subject. She had respected my wishes, and in all our work around my inherited Holocaust trauma, she had kept herself, her valuing of tradition and Jewish community, out of it.

At the funeral, I felt I was hearing about a stranger, someone I'd hardly met except to have been introduced to in passing. It reinforced what I had sensed from the moment I descended into the adjunct premises within which she so skillfully plied her trade, that her work derived from a place in her being that was quite separate from the rest of her life, not just in that it protected her private world from her patients' struggles, but a place her own, as much as it was for those who sought her care. I wanted to speak. Me with my reluctance to address an audience. I wanted to get up there to say there was another side to her. Perhaps it wasn't the biggest part. Perhaps it was tiny in relation to the rest—her family, her synagogue, and her collegial and cultural affiliations. But it was vital, shining below stairs through the dirt raised by our disrupted lives, a brilliance that was her quietude and gift of repair.

We left the chapel with her voice in our ears, a recording of her singing a liturgical tune. She had a beautiful singing voice, something, again, I couldn't have foreseen. The evanescence of those pure notes wrung the last drops out of me. "How did you know her? Are you family or friend?" the mourner beside me asked as I wadded up my sodden tissues. "I didn't," I said. "I was a patient."

* * *

There would have come a point when she could no longer read my letters. Family members would have had to vet her correspondence. Perhaps they put them aside, afraid they might hold something that could upset her, or maybe she asked for them to be read aloud. I'll never know, and it doesn't matter. I had wanted to give her something even those who lovingly looked after her didn't have in them to give. I wanted her to know that the healer in her continued to be present to me, and that on some level her work went on, I went on, carrying our work in me, keeping her professional light alive. I wrote that she might think I was seeking her in my new man, John, replacing her through him, and that maybe she'd be right and maybe there was nothing actually wrong with that.

It was she who had triggered the moment that had brought us together. We'd stood in the kitchen clearing away dishes after a Sunday dinner. Separated from his wife, John tried to fill weekends with routine diversions. He noted I was unusually quiet. And I'd said, "It's my doctor. She's on her way out." I couldn't say the d-word anymore. He'd put his arms around me, dishcloth still in hand. We all wish our dead could see the outcome of the years they missed out on, and I wish that she could see how my life has opened with John.

In his anguish over his father, my sixteen-year-old had cried, "He'll never know how I turned out, what I end up becoming." More poignant because he himself hadn't yet known. When Craig died, she invited me to bring my son along to my next session, if I thought it might help. You make it up as you go when norms don't fit. My sister thought otherwise. "Why re-invent the wheel? People over the millennia made road maps; that's what rituals are. You think you have to hack your way through the bush." Yes, I did. It was my right to cut my own path from the land of a living Craig to the new world of Craig dead. My therapist didn't question this, but suggested instead that I bring along my son.

Sixteen, too young to know he couldn't yet grasp everything, but old enough to get that one fact was all, the fact of no father. The fact that altered all others. He came and we took a southerly route to avoid his high school, reminder of all that was usual but no longer so for him. We drove through the Rosedale Valley instead. It was May, three years prior to when she herself would be buried. Each acid green leaf was a piercing affront. My son stared out the open window, letting the wind slash him like a cat only half in play.

Before we reached the waiting room, she emerged from her office. She had been listening for our footfalls. She clasped my hands, squeezing hard. With a heart-leap of gratitude, I saw she was already looking over my shoulder to the boy who towered over us both. I would learn at her funeral that she had two sons herself. But she was looking then at my son, seeing him in his loss, and seeing in him her own sons as they might have grieved for her had she not recovered from the grave illness I was not yet aware of. Seeing in my wounded son what I would later see in hers. She led him by the elbow ever so gently. Inside the office, she pressed his large hand between both of her palms. He met her clear regard, giving up nothing. Her tone was respectfully formal as it was tender. "I'm very sorry for your loss." My son dipped his tousled head and intuitively took the third chair she had put in place. We spoke in low voices, she and I, about this and that. My son answered when addressed, politely disengaged. It wasn't a session, but a *shiva* visit in reverse. She paid court to our loss, just as if we, principal mourners, had been sitting on the floor of our own living room in the age-old observance of bereavement. Craig at this point was not so much missed, but a stunning, unassimilable absence. We didn't know who we were without him, or what shape our lives might take. Her voice, neutral and profoundly onside, indicated she understood.

In the misbegotten future, I would search art shops and galleries for something to give her, an object in glass—hollow, exquisitely fragile, no larger than my fist.

Life After Death

MY SECOND HUSBAND AND I rocked the boat when we got together, his ex-wife my cousin. Our great-grandmothers, in a late, eradicated world, had been sisters. John and I went to see their fin de siècle childhood home, the Zukermann manor in northeastern Hungary. Like everything in that puny, puffed-up state, the house was small by comparison to its place in family lore. Mansard roof and gables notwithstanding, it would look dwarfed set against the North American inflations of both families' later generations.

The blood we inadvertently left in the waters at the start of our relationship wasn't just my cousin's. Their marriage had been crumbling for years; my part was only in its dismantling. She and John had intended to wait out the summer, at which point their youngest would join their eldest at university, and then the parents would set their minds on how best to dissolve both their marriage and home with a minimum of turbulence. But one of their discussions had veered off course, disclosing our relationship before they'd settled on a plan. Within days, my cousin had bought herself a house; within a week of that, so had John and I. The movers took charge a month later.

As they started removing the boxes I'd packed, sealed, and labelled over the last weeks, as they picked up the furniture from one room and then the other, my eldest found refuge under the raised bed in his brother's tiny room that had originally been set up by previous owners as a nursery. Tall and big-boned, at his full growth but scrunched into a ball, he looked, when I happened on him there, as though he too were crated. I'd always sheltered my kids from the worst. Certainly, I'd shielded them from the knowledge of their father's chronic mental illness as much as I had Craig himself, and let's not forget me, twenty-five-year obfuscator of the daily manifestations of Craig's anxiety and self-loathing depression. My instinct had been to spare my kids as much as I could, which meant in this case they hadn't had to help prepare the house for sale or pack up their rooms. I had never taught them to cook, clean, take out the garbage, or pick up milk when we ran out. While the movers worked, Zachary burrowed under his brother's bed, nursing a state of shock.

I had packed things systematically for a month, while John's family threw things around, out, and into boxes. Setting up our new household later in the summer, I'd find boxes marked Dad's shit, Dad's fucking crap, and so on. They, unlike me, had taught their kids to lend a hand.

Moving day started in a semblance of order with my house first. By afternoon, the movers took my cousin's belongings to her new place. Only later did they get around to John's. Later, as in early evening, they had to empty a rented storage unit as well as the rest of John and my cousin's house. John's kids hadn't weeded things out. In one box, for instance, I would find the contents of a wastepaper basket. Furnishings started stacking up willy-nilly. The humid buildup of the August day finally broke into rain as darkness loomed. My strapping big boy, beloved and coddled first child, saw that help was required. He lugged stuff up numerous flights of stairs, up and down for the next three hours, his mouth locked in a rictus of determination and rage. This is the look I will forever associate with collateral damage. It distorted the faces of all our four children at one point or another as they struggled to adjust to a situation entirely not of their making, nor to their liking. When the spent movers finally settled onto the porch with a bottle of whiskey John had brought out, Zachary continued to toil, hauling boxes to approximate locations.

"Zack, tomorrow's a new day. The rest can wait," I said.

"Maybe for you," he snapped. "A happy day for the rest of us, my ass."

"Zachary," John intervened. And that was it. The big, tall bulk of my boy sank to the floor as though felled by an axe.

"He used a father's voice," he cried. "I know what a father's voice sounds like, but he isn't my father. I have no father!"

Anger, anguish, exhaustion overflowed for hours on the new ceramic tile, while he sobbed against the refrigerator door. My boy, whom I'd always tried to spare but had pierced now with a bitter arrow. He'd banked on me doing the work of mourning, much as I'd relieved him of chores around the house. I'd been waiting four years since his father's death for Zachary to face his grief. Naturally, this would be the night.

* * *

During the period of our trysts, John's work had often taken him away. I bought a cellphone so he could reach me anytime. No one else had the number. It was always with me, as I didn't know when it might ring, especially when John was in a different time zone. I jumped to its chiming ditty like Pavlov's dog. Heart pounding, I'd drop what I was doing. If the phone rang on a secondary highway as I was driving my youngest to an out-of-town tournament, I'd pull a hard right onto the shoulder and scamper out. I have no idea who my child thought I needed to talk to so urgently by the side of the road. John brought the world to me from New York, Vilnius, Colombo. Foreign traffic sounded in the background as he walked along describing architectural features. It felt plentiful, entirely satisfying to be brought into the scene through his voice.

I'd forgotten that I had ever considered myself well-travelled, something I'd boast about as a child who'd logged more travel miles than any of her friends in the sixties and seventies, even though my family had never owned a car. Many of these places I'd travelled to on my own by Greyhound or airplane: Boston, New York, Syracuse, Philadelphia, Washington, D.C., San Francisco. A few relatives from the Diaspora had washed up, like us, on the shores of the new world, and these families opened their doors to one another just as the lost dozens in my parents' families had clung clannishly to one another through thick and, lastly, perilously thin.

I was ten-and-a-half the first time my father put me on a Greyhound by myself in Montreal's bus terminal next to Central Station. I'd woken with excitement in my Ville d'Anjou bedroom on the morning of travel, knowing that by evening I'd be eating in my cousin's wainscotted dining room with its matching walnut plate rail. Compared to my family's suburban new-build, my cousin's large old house in upstate New York felt exhilaratingly exotic. I loved the smell of that house. Had it been edible, I'd have shovelled it in. I don't know if it came from the cleanser that Zsuzsa, my cousin's mom, used, or her laundry soap, or if she put sachets of herbs into the drawers and cupboards, as later she'd make sachets so my little boys would have sweet dreams. As soon as I ran from the carport into the tiny, white kitchen steaming with the aroma of a simmering dinner, I'd sniff deeply for the distinctive scent below the one drifting from the stove. It was in Zsuzsa's apron, on her skin, in the air. It would float out of every closet I'd open, even from within the piano bench. It was the heavenly scent of indulgences and treats that my withholding mother wouldn't have dreamed of offering.

When John brought the world to me, I had no expectation of ever getting out into it myself. Interests from my younger days had been on hold for so long, I'd stopped missing them. Craig and I took one overseas trip after our first year together. I'd thought it might help him shake the web of gloom that had adhered to every part of his system, a sticky coagulant that had kept him gummed up, unable to train for a marathon, play tennis, read novels, or write stories—offsets to the effort it took for him to get out of bed. The trip hadn't transformed him, but it did get him vertical. Travelling with Craig had been like carrying an extra backpack.

John and I were in our new house hardly longer than six weeks before he suggested I join him on his trip to Vancouver where he would be attending a conference. My eldest had just begun university, and my youngest starting high school. At the top of Whistler Mountain, my cellphone, now the line everyone used, went off. "Oh, Josh, sweetie, you wouldn't believe what I'm looking at. The most gorgeous . . ."

His voice cut me off. "Where's the glue stick?" he said flatly, uninterested in anything his troublesome mother might be up to after disrupting his life, plunking him in a big new house, and promptly taking off without telling him where she'd stashed the stationery supplies. Little did I realize that John would propose two more trips attached to work-related projects before year end, one to Europe and the other to Asia. He said carpe diem, but to me it felt more like making up for lost time.

After a few days in Budapest, my place of birth, we rented a Škoda, and with John at the wheel and an ancient cousin of my father's bent double in the front seat, we undertook a pilgrimage into the northeast to track down the erstwhile landmarks of my father's once-prolific family. My relative, Ági, eighty-three years of age, suffered from chronic pain and had difficulty moving around. Still, she was keen to return to the countryside of her youth where she had formed her happiest memories.

First, I wanted to see the Rákóczi estate where my father had grown up. The only structure left standing, though, was the little station hut lined in rambling rose wallpaper. It had been erected before the turn of the century, when my great-grandfather Jakab had succeeded in bribing the railroad into making stops at the estate to pick up its shipments of tobacco and alcohol. Here, visitors would disembark on a regular basis. Ági said she used to count the stations leading up to the Rákóczi stop. The hut still felt like a little fairy-tale house, a single small room with a bench on either side, a small hearth on one end, and the door on the other. An excited young girl from the big city, she'd try to spot the first sighting of the hut that signalled the outpouring of love and attention she'd enjoy in my grandparents' household of three boys.

I stroked the peeling wallpaper. Had the grandmother I knew only from my father's anecdotes chosen the pattern, or her own mother, dead in her prime from a ruptured appendix? Nearby, we toured the seat of the count who'd leased the lands to my grandfather and who'd offered, during the war, to adopt my father's pretty little niece so that she wouldn't get carted away with the rest of them if the Nazis went back on their word and occupied the country after all.

In Nyiregyháza, we walked up and down a street without sidewalks until Ági was satisfied that she had picked out the exact stuccoed bungalow my father had lived in with his first wife, Mancika, and their little daughter, Évike. He had kept the accounts for the family business from his office in this bungalow, and, after he'd escaped slave labour service to the Hungarian army, it was from the dirt of this street that he'd scooped up some of the family photos and correspondence that had been tossed out when interlopers helped themselves to the premises.

In Varsány, we couldn't believe our luck in finding the house of John's former mother-in-law, our cousin Zsuzsa, still in use and occupied by a couple who carved, of all things, gravestones. After some reluctance and under-the-breath mutterings about 'knowing nothing' regarding what had gone on before their time, they let us in to look around. Zsuzsa and her murdered brother's nursery was the room of the teenaged son, now lined with posters of rock bands. They asked us not to take pictures, but I knew that Zsuzsa would have found it too painful anyway to see the cherished room her memory had preserved, now so radically transformed. As we were leaving, an aged man in a sleeveless undershirt stood waiting at the car. He gave us a snapshot of the outside of the house taken for the local historical society. "There was a little girl who liked to visit the stables," he said, and then quickly turned away.

The Kisvárda Synagogue's walled-in grounds had been the site of the first internment camp my father's loved ones had been deported to. A discreet commemorative plaque hung on the locked gate of what is now a museum. We'd arrived after business hours. I can't remember how John and I found our way into the grounds, while Ági waited on a bench outside. It felt as desolate as the empty schoolyards of my childhood. My sister would drop me off in the mornings before catching the bus to her high school, my parents having left for work much earlier. No matter how often I was dropped off at the same time, I'd fret during the long minutes before others would dribble in, certain I was late, the bell having already rung while I continued truant.

By the time we drove by the Mansard-roofed Zukermann house, family home of my father's and Zsuzsa's grandmothers, we were weary, as much if not more from our passage through a landscape of shades as the many hours on the go. Waning light was a concern. And Ági was very tired. Her loud voice had not stopped talking since we'd left Budapest at eight that morning. It was a grating voice, and Ági herself was draining, deeply immersed in a vocalized stream of consciousness that, though often informative, jarred. We were looking for the last site, the family cemetery, most incongruous of conceits. Some of us— of them—had actually succeeded in making a timely escape by dying before the deportations.

According to Ági, the family cemetery in Lövö had still existed when she had last sought it out with my sister, surviving both the war and Soviet makeovers of the countryside. Originally meant to accommodate the many-branched clan, a smattering of family members lay under the earth, marked by actual headstones. At the time, I couldn't have said why it felt so pressing to visit these graves. Now, I think it's because there are no others. No markers to remember our lost family, nor the hundreds of thousands or millions, save the unholy spires of Auschwitz and its iconic gates to hell. No epitaphs mark their memories other than "Work Will Set You Free."

We drove along the road that led out of the town past the Zukermann house.

"It's just along here." Ági leaned as far forward as her bent torso permitted. "On the left side."

In the back, I shuffled over to the driver's side to peer out. Copses, brushy verges. John turned the car around, and we inched along back the way we'd come, scouring the roadside.

"It must be here. I saw it with Elaine," said Ági. My sister had visited a decade earlier.

Dusk had fallen as we drove up the quiet country road once more.

"John, let's give it up. It's late, and we've run out of light." I didn't think I could bear any more of Ági's raucous cry, "It's here. I know it is. I know it is." I was sick of my family's claims to know everything. Each of us was a know-it-all, and how had that worked out?

John didn't come from the same fatalistic stock. He turned the car crossways to face the side of the road, levelling the high beams into the brush. "Did you see that?" he asked, straining his eyes over the dashboard. He pulled the car over at an angle, aiming the lights at what he thought he'd glimpsed. I helped Ági to the roadside as John leapt out. Over a ditch and into blackness. "Oh gosh," we heard him call. Then we heard him rustle back to readjust the car so that the light might better pick out what he'd found. Ági, bent, fragile, aching with both pain and heartbreak, breathed out a quiet, "Yes," as her feet somehow remembered a former nimbleness.

There were tombstones, not many, most of them atilt or toppled, reclaimed by weeds and grasses. I searched within the blinding glare and in the shadows beyond the range of the brights for the one my sister had told me about, the stone our father had described of his grandfather Jakab, widower with thirteen children. Jakab had expanded the family farm into an agronomical enterprise. He'd brought the first telephone into the county, the first car, the first mechanized tractor. An innovator and great spendthrift who could deny his children nothing. I ran my hands along the faces of the few standing headstones, until I felt his, engraved with the candelabra of thirteen branches. Thirteen branches of blood lines, more than eighty among them taken to slaughter.

Oh, the sweet richness and profligate sentiment of a doting father and the world in which it had made a difference. John took my hand. My big sister's scolding remark when she first heard that John and I had fallen in love echoed back to me: "What you think is love is some post-traumatic peccadillo." Censure had come from others as well. One long-standing friend had landed a swift sabre thrust. "Seeing as how Craig already killed himself, all you need is for your cousin to do the same and away you go." Hand-in-hand, John and I bent our heads. We'd take the blessing where we might find it, from the song of the stones.

One spirals around and back even as one moves forward, a twister that picks up and tosses off, only to retrieve the same bit of debris as it carves a path. Each winter of my childhood, I'd rip open the birthday parcel Zsuzsa would send me by mail, knowing it would be filled with my cousin's lightly used hand-me-downs that would still be in fashion, unlike those from my sister who was six years older. Opening the box, I also found books, fabric scraps, and sewing notions I'd use for outfitting my Barbie dolls, all exuding a clean, unsweet, vaguely herbal odour, the distinctive pheromone of their old house that touched off in me a kind of olfactory swoon.

How to convey why one loves? A force, perhaps not dissimilar to the one that drove my father to my mother, my mother to my father after war stole their everyones, may have quickened me, too. Emotional wounds still oozing—as they would, off and on, for the rest of their lives—they'd leapt at a chance for life after death.

One morning, three years after Craig died, I was seized by a desire to unmake the bed I'd just put together. I tore back the linens, threw them about, and left them like that for the rest of the day. I started the rewrite of my story before I knew what I was doing. When a flicker, iridescent with promise darted over the page, I snatched at it like a trout at a fly.

Postcards from the Land of the Oppressors

THE FIRST NAZI WAR crimes trial, the Belsen Trial, had been held by the British in the town of Lüneburg, Lower Saxony, from September 17 to November 17, 1945. On trial were men and women of the SS, as well as *kapos*, prisoners in supervisory roles, from Auschwitz and the Bergen-Belsen concentration camp located barely eighty kilometres away. We arrived in Lüneburg on April 19, 2015, coinciding to the week seventy years earlier that the British had liberated Bergen-Belsen. Repeatedly, we heard that Lüneburg had held the first Nazi trial and might well be hosting the last.

I'd read that after liberating Bergen-Belsen, the British had forced the citizens of a nearby town to view what had taken place on their doorstep. The town was actually the village of Celle, which was sixteen kilometres from the camp, but I didn't know this when we arrived in Lüneburg. As John and I stepped out of our quaint inn built around the original front wall of the town's historic market hall, I wondered if it had been Lüneburg's population that had been trucked in to the camp to witness the shameful conditions they had lived in close proximity to and yet denied. I gazed across the Ilmenau River to the medieval crane for loading salt onto barges that had sailed down the Ilmenau to the Elbe and on to the Baltic. Lüneburg was one of the few towns in Germany to have survived the war largely intact, and its preserved condition brought in tourists from all over the country. The distinctive stepped-gable facades of the guildhalls and burgers *hauses*, varicoloured and decorated with folkloric motifs, had been immaculately maintained. Late blooms glinted in the greening forsythia, while on the boulevard, pink flowering almond was a-puff. Though leafed out, the willows on the river bank still rippled with newly minted shimmer. The ancient buildings, built on the salt dome from which the town had drawn its wealth, were gradually sinking into it. They tipped picturesquely one into the next.

Thomas Walther had asked those among the co-plaintiffs who were able to do so to arrive a couple of days before the start of the trial. His plan was to hold a media event to capitalize on the public's thirst for personal stories. I assumed John and I would join the co-plaintiffs, their companions, and Thomas's team over a dinner or two, but that after most days in court, we'd be free to explore on our own. It's unlikely any of the co-plaintiffs were prepared for the total immersion that awaited: the cameras at the airport, interviews at the hotel, attendance at official functions. A woman in her late eighties who had travelled on the plane with us from Toronto was whisked away from the airport in a media van with her daughter and her luggage, and she was interviewed throughout the seventy-minute ride to Lüneburg. When she stepped out in front of the hotel, she smiled wanly at the other journalists waiting in line. Her daughter asked for a half-hour reprieve, but the determined mother said, "No, it's fine. I'll be down in fifteen minutes." So it began.

My role as second generation was at most a supporting one, yet it would draw on my reserves. I could only imagine the rigours demanded of these aged women and men who were requested numerous times each day to repeat the dreadful story of their young lives. I would hear from a few of them that for decades, they had barely spoken a word outside their families about their Holocaust past. Now they faced reporters from news outlets all over the world asking them to share ever more.

The atmosphere in the courtroom was fittingly subdued despite the milling of the media with their equipment. Out of doors, the verdant lawns and outdoor patios, filled with patrons even this early in the season, evoked a sense of event and liveliness. The subject that had drawn us together was one of the most macabre in human history, yet those here to tell the decades-old tale of deprivation and loss suffered first-hand looked remarkably well for their age. They exuded energy and resilience. A few days into the trial, a couple of them arrived straight from taking part in a March of the Living to Dachau. They couldn't have been more 'living': motivated and thriving, the progenitors of multi-generational families. These participants were obviously the youngest and strongest of the surviving Holocaust cohort, impelled by a drive not to let the world forget the atrocities committed against them and their loved ones. They were no less remarkable for their perseverance.

While we had been gathered here by million-fold deaths, a restored, vibrant Germany had given rise to the occasion. If the country had not been thriving, the third post-war generation probably would not have been willing to engage in an inquiry into the crimes of their forebears. Distance through time, economic stability, and regained strength combined to create a zone of safety in which both the victim and the perpetrator could look back.

The war had taken a huge toll on Germany. Most of the Germans we met, non-Jews, found it difficult to speak of their families' losses or suffering. There was a striking tourist feature in Berlin, which we visited on a long weekend. In the downtown Mitte district, giant 'books' of black-and-white photographs constituted both historic record and public art. One could see, as one flipped the plexiglass pages, what the spot one was standing on, as well as various views from it, had looked like at the end of the war. These photos spoke to the single-minded national effort that had gone into reconstruction: physical reconstruction first, and cultural/ spiritual/psychological reconstruction coming later.

We were given another kind of snapshot of the nation's passage through stages of post-war transition by a filmmaker who was tracking Thomas through his mission. We met over coffee while waiting for her cameraman. She wanted to know my story, but I was curious about hers. Modestly, she opted to discuss the country. Her main interest was 'perpetration,' and Germany was a fitting subject. "But," John interrupted, "there were war crimes on both sides even if the Allies weren't brought to account for theirs." She appeared immediately uncomfortable. "The firebombing of Dresden is the best example," he persisted, "but so many German cities were subjected to British Air Marshal 'Bomber' Harris's preference for area bombing over strategic, target bombing, which even at the time was considered questionable. His deliberate destruction of civilian populations fits my idea of a war crime." Our friend struggled to reply. Her English was excellent, so her loss of words was due to uneasiness.

"I cannot speak about this," she said finally.

"It is not possible," John asked, "because as a person of conscience you identify with the victims?"

She recovered and clarified, "Here in Germany, only the Holocaust deniers and those who try to make excuses for the Nazis talk this way."

We bumped into our new friend more than once, and each time we resumed the thread of our conversation. "In the first generation that lived through the war and had to pick up afterwards, the important thing was to survive, work, feed their families, and rebuild the country. Rebuilding, reconstruction, I would say, was the collective aim of the nation immediately post-war. Then in the next generation, Thomas's, born at the war's end or soon after, there was a new dimension. This was the generation of the 1968 student movements. Much attention everywhere was on the politics of liberation, anti-war, and focus on minority rights. Here in Germany, naturally, this movement got us thinking about Germany's human rights abuses, in particular, as the most obvious example, against the Jews. And so you have this next generation looking at financial restitution for the victims, and focusing on the victims by building museums and memorials. But still, no one wanted to look too closely at ourselves, those at home who took part in the war. No one was asking 'what did papa or grandpapa or mama do in the war?' Not until now, the third generation. Now there are groups organized to help people research their own families and relatives. Now we are finally prepared to start looking at ourselves, but it takes time, distance, this long, three generations, seventy years."

"And," I added, "all the buildings restored, industries rebuilt, farms and gardens re-cultivated, everything in bloom." We smiled at the spring trees.

"Yes, certainly," she agreed, "only when we have full bellies do we find energy for thinking about who we are and where we have come from and why we do what we do."

I suggested that the world could look to Germany as an example of how long it could take to make meaningful amends when it came to seeking truth and reconciliation between perpetrators and victims. Indigenous peoples and their colonizers, Palestinians and Israelis, Hutus and Tutsis, Serbs and Croats, Afrikaners and Blacks, Iraqis, Turks, and Kurds, Chechens and Russians, Sunnis and Shiites, and Syrians and Syrians: the list went on. Some of these conflicts had concluded, and the sides sought resolutions they could abide. In some instances, villagers who once murdered each other's close kin had to continue living side by side. Truth and reconciliation commissions had been set up to seek justice for injured parties, and alternative strategies of restorative justice had also been tested in close environments. There was a pressing need to fix relations before violence erupted again, but it was important to keep in perspective what could be reasonably achieved. In that way, I said, the example of Germany was useful. We could note what had succeeded, initiatives that had proved constructive, and what had gone awry. Germany was the rare example of a nation that had undertaken to come to grips with its history of perpetrating genocide by formal acknowledgement of its role, financial restitution, and education of the new generations as to what had gone on under Nazi rule. The trial of Oskar Gröning was critical in this respect. One more lost piece of the shattered structure had been found, giving rise to the opportunity to hammer it back into place.

* * *

In court, we learned that the German legal system was not like ours. The case was tried by five judges, three of them professionally trained and certified and two of them lay judges selected from the public. There was no jury. The professional judges wore robes, as did the prosecutor and attorneys. I noted with surprise that one of the lay judges had shown up in a hoodie and khakis. The next day he wore jeans. The court reporter had her own self-styled uniform, jeans tucked into mid-calf tan boots, with a crisp white blouse, its collar open. The journalists in the main were relaxed in dress as well. Even the defendant wore a woollen jersey vest over a soft checked shirt, as though he were at home reading his newspaper by the fire. On Thursday, the court disbanded for the weekend. After session, the court officers would jump into their cars for the drive home on the *autobahns*. Thomas's jeans showed beneath his robe, as did one judge's red slacks. I wondered if I could read into the dress code more than met the eye.

Could it be a sign of the deliberate attempts within the culture to distance itself from the paternalistic, authoritarian values and practices that had given rise to the National Socialists, with its emphasis on regimentation, order, and discipline expressed in buttoned-down uniforms and formal attire? The Germans of today seemed hell-bent on looking laid back.

It shocked me, also, to find the language sounded pleasant. I had yet to hear a single barking order or the harsh intonations Hollywood movies had led me to expect. I felt a sudden longing to speak German in order to read the reports of the journalists who interviewed us, or listen in on our lawyers' gossipy murmurs over drinks. Especially, I'd have loved to hear the testimonies in the original. Simultaneous translation of court proceedings was spotty. On my headset, I flipped back and forth between English and Hungarian. The Hungarian was often easier to follow, although my Hungarian is limited to a young child's kitchen vocabulary. In German, as in Hungarian, the verb comes at the end of the sentence. The poor English translators piled up the clauses waiting for the German verb, but when it arrived, they often missed it, because the speaker had already launched the next sentence. In their struggle to keep up, meaning was often lost.

This was not the case with the Burgermeister's speech when we convened for a reception hosted by city hall. The reception was held in the Heinrich Heine Haus, so called because the poet's parents had resided here during the mid-1820s, and he had visited often. The handsomely restored sixteenth-century patrician's home was originally built for the master artisan of the saltworks. Perhaps it had been chosen as the site for our reception because Heine's family remained Jewish while Heine himself became a Lutheran as an adult. The house made a gracious, intimate setting for a small reception. I had expected to hear a pro forma official address from the Burgermeister welcoming us to Lüneburg as a duty of his office. Instead, I was moved by the lyricism and openness of his words, which came through even in translation. His personal presentation lifted the whole into a convincing statement on behalf of the town:

> "It pains me that nowadays, many people still do not want to come to terms with this problem.
>
> "It pains me that there are still people who deny the Shoah and other crimes committed during the Nazi era.
>
> "It pains me that there are persons who seem to believe that the crime is less grave the greater the number of victims. Even one victim is one too many.
>
> "It pains me that there are people marching through our towns shouting slogans in public full of hatred, still in favour of the Nazis."

By then, day four of the trial, I should have been used to conversations that cut to the chase. At dinner on the first evening, we had already abandoned small talk. The day that had started out for some of us on another continent had required our talking to strangers on personal subjects. The point of this exercise was to put real faces to the astronomical figures of the anonymous dead. The reporters wanted to know how the survivors had felt as they were deported. When was the last time they had seen their mother? Father? Baby sister? Had they ever given up hope or wished to die? I, too, had been questioned. At dinner, with little social reservation left, the group went straight to discussing the main issues raised by the trial. It would be the same all week. Whether talking to a lawyer on our team or to a journalist either on or off the record, one strove for an emotionally authentic exchange.

* * *

In our Berlin hotel room, John flipped channels, curious about local broadcasting while keeping an eye out for BBC World. I was Skyping with a BBC online editor in London who would be publishing my testimony after I read it in court. My son in Toronto had scanned and sent the editor photos of my half-sister and her mother, and one photo of my father and his two brothers in the uniform of slave labourers assigned to the Hungarian military. Our conversation took a turn to the personal as had so many over the last week. This editor, whose surname was Irish, told me his mother was a Dutch Jewish survivor of the war who had only recently been able to bring herself to visit her home village from which most of the Jews had been deported.

Scratch the surface in Europe and barely beneath the topmost layer one encountered the war. This explained the extent of media coverage of the trial from almost every corner of Europe. Our lawyers represented a total of fifty-five co-plaintiffs, fourteen of whom were presenting testimony in Lüneburg. Twenty-one of the total came from Canada, as did seven of the fourteen who would give testimony. Not a single representative of the Canadian media was in attendance. A schism from my childhood reopened. The response on the part of our Canadian acquaintances to my parents' accents and implicit tragic past had been to look away, as though these were somehow in bad form, not to be acknowledged in polite society. It was hard not to take personally, not to feel that their losses had become embarrassingly non-topical. Being asked here to tell the stories of our families so publicly had a liberating effect on many of us co-plaintiffs.

I joined John on the sofa in front of the TV, drawn by a familiar voice speaking English. Before we'd left Lüneburg for the break, we had heard the testimony of an American Auschwitz survivor, Eva Cor. As ten-year-old twins in Auschwitz, she and her sister had been subjected to the medical experiments of Josef Mengele. Her testimony, as it related to this experience, was beyond difficult to listen to. Her testimony was noteworthy in other respects, too. She used the occasion to publicize her views on the healing power of forgiveness and to promote an organization she had founded to help survivors of trauma move forward through the practice of forgiveness. These were controversial ideas to air among former death camp internees, as one may surmise, but her act upon leaving the courtroom created more of a stir. As she walked by Oskar Gröning, Mrs. Cor stopped to take his hand, speak with him, and give him a hug.

Mrs. Cor had found a strategy that had helped her put aside her hatred and build a life around a constructive principle. While this might be admired, her plugging her message as from a soapbox at this particular venue, giving offence to other Auschwitz survivors and distracting from the business at hand, which was to establish legal guilt, was hurtful and counterproductive. Her provocative behaviour in the courtroom was quickly picked up by the media. Here she sat on a panel on German public television, along with four other speakers. We recognized a journalist who was in the courtroom each day, a woman of strong presence, and another familiar face, the second chair defence attorney for Oskar Gröning, whom I had seen wiping her eyes during Mrs. Cor's account of her childhood torture. But even Mrs. Cor's English was drowned out by the German translator. We watched the incomprehensible discussion for a few minutes and then gave up in frustration.

On our return to Lüneburg, our friend, the filmmaker, asked if we'd like to watch the panel discussion on her iPad while she translated. What luck. The show was a weekly with a moderator, she said, who liked to stir controversies. Mrs. Cor's hugging the former Nazi had given rise to debate. The journalist we'd recognized was from *Der Spiegel*, and was known for her in-depth articles. The federal minister of justice was also on the panel, as well as a Jewish historian and a war historian. The first thing that struck me was the personal tone of the speakers. Even the minister of justice spoke as the Burgermeister had, as an individual rather than a public representative.

The *Der Spiegel* journalist spontaneously shared an intimate family experience. Recently, she and her mother had gone on a pilgrimage to Auschwitz. Jews organize Marches of the Living to keep Jewish youth apprised of the history of their forebears and to ensure that the slogan, "Never Again!" remained meaningful to upcoming generations. But not only Jews paid their respects to the dead of the death camps. When the journalist and her mother stepped through the infamous gates with the grimly ironic dictum, "Work Will Set You Free," the journalist said her mother withdrew into herself. Entering a detention block, she broke into tears. The journalist was puzzled by the intensity of this response. "I see your father here," her mother finally explained. Her father? Here? The journalist had been baffled. She had never heard that her father, a native German, had ever been held in Auschwitz. "Yes, he was here. He suffered here too, a political prisoner."

It was a piece of personal history the journalist's parents had kept from her all her life until now in her middle years, germane information about her father that she might have been proud of. "I remembered all the times my father had surprised me," she said. "Once, a policeman stopped him for a traffic offence, and my father very violently struck the policeman's hand from his shoulder. Other times, too, he seemed to overreact to a provocation. Now I understood." Although her father had shared some of the fate of the Auschwitz Jews, he had not felt it was his right to claim a territory of suffering; he, after all, belonged to the nation of the perpetrators. I was struck again by the frankness of the discussion. Perhaps the culture that had fallen for such a huge lie in the past put more emphasis now on talking straight.

* * *

Oskar Gröning was convicted of accessory to murder on 300,000 counts in July 2015, the charge upheld by the appeals court almost a year later. He was sentenced to four years in prison but died in 2018 before serving any time. Reinhold Hanning was convicted of 170,000 counts of aiding and abetting murder in June 2016. He died before the appeals court had reached a decision, and before serving time. Since then, other former concentration camp and death march guards have been charged, but because of their deterioration both mentally and physically due to advanced age, verdicts upheld post-appeal have proved as elusive as in the cases of Demjanjuk and Hanning. This is why the outcome of the Gröning trial was so significant. It was the first case in which the full legal process was completed—charges, trial, and appeal. It established, and confirmed on appeal, that anyone who had participated in the application of The Final Solution was, by extension, guilty of aiding and abetting murder.

Conflict resolution depends on two principles: accountability and recognition of injury. To be equitable, these principles must apply on both sides of the equation. A recurring image from my childhood hovers at the back of my mind whenever I contemplate my postcard impressions from the land of the oppressors. My mother often recounted how she and my aunt, her younger sister, had journeyed across Germany and Central Europe, trying to find their way back to Hungary. By then they had been moved from Auschwitz, eventually ending up on a death march to Dresden. In the chaos following their liberation by the Americans, they wended their circuitous way homewards. At the time it had been difficult to tell friend from foe. As a listening child, I couldn't understand why their flight had to be so furtive; wasn't all of Europe now liberated, from the east by the Russians and from the west by the Allies? What I remember from her accounts are two details. How they managed to dig a potato out of the ground and keep it warm against their skin for days, to soften and slow cook. A child who'd loved to eat would remember such an image. The other was what a girl of any age would react to. "We had to hide in the forest and walk only at night, because the Russians raped anything female that stirred."

The Russian ravaging of German lands and women had been so total, the very forest creatures must have hissed with the news. No one was saying the Germans hadn't killed over twenty-five million people during their siege of Russia, of which but a third had been military. No one was saying the Germans had been the good guys. Forgiveness was the last thing on my mind when I thought of a Nazi, even an aged one in a woollen vest and shirt open at the neck. Forgiveness, though, should not be confused with bearing witness to loss, devastation, pain, and distress. My mother and my aunt, slaves of the Nazi camp system, had yet been terrified of falling into the hands of the Russians and suffering the fate of German women.

* * *

Daily in Lüneburg, I was taken for a representative of the Jewish community. Together, we co-plaintiffs filed off the coach hired to take us to court and strolled processionally into the building as cameras tailed us on caddies. Microphones swaddled in microfibre muffs hung over our heads to pick up remarks we learned to keep to ourselves. We sat side by side in the courtroom and moved as one to the adjoining hall during adjournments when journalists once more swarmed to our honey. We were the co-plaintiffs, Jews all, seemingly homogeneous.

What made me uncomfortable among Jews were assumptions that we shared values just because we were Jews. I felt deeply offended when conclusions were drawn not just about me because I'd been born and raised Jewish, but about the incontestable merit of certain principles that allegedly defined us because of history and lineage: that a good Jew supported Israel at any cost, even if not its one state policy, or that a good Jew practised cultural traditions because not doing so furthered the Nazis' aim to eradicate us all—that whatever the cause we should stick together. I didn't buy it, but I was equally Jewish.

Before leaving for Germany, I had worried as much about being part of a group of Jews as I had about being surrounded by Germans. Had it not been for Thomas Walther and the Gröning trial, I would never have crossed the border into the land where my mother and aunt had been slaves. Because of this German man, I strove to also overcome my aversion to being absorbed into a collective of my own kind. It felt like an achievement to separate the survivor voices of the courtroom from some of the statements they made at our dinners and breakfasts, often fierce in antipathy to Palestinians and other Arabs. Evidently one could feel respect, compassion, and even affection for the person who had suffered unspeakably, while finding his or her politics distasteful. It still dismayed me, though, whenever one of the group presumed that it was natural to agree that one who questioned Israel was its enemy, and that the Holocaust justified disenfranchisement of those not our kind. These positions cheapened the tragedy of the Shoah.

In Lüneberg, I surprised myself by extending a level of patience and support to survivors that I had offered only in comparatively niggardly proportions to my mother and my aunt. Perhaps by my solicitude, I actually meant to say thanks to my mother for her bravery, perseverance, and her leap of faith in giving birth to us, and sorry to them both for once being a royal pain. They were both very old by that time. My aunt, ninety-five, came to my sister's home for dinner whenever I was in Montreal. She sat beside me, patted my hand, and told me she wouldn't pass up the chance because, "Tu sais, je t'aime beaucoup." I doubted she took seriously—if she remembered it at all—the time she once chewed me out over an old antimacassar. I too had let it go. My mother, ninety-six, was cognitively compromised. Maybe that was why she could say I was beautiful. The thought would never have crossed her mind, let alone her lips, when I was young and insecure in my womanhood. I chose to believe she was freer at this stage to speak her heart. I could accept the compliment as a gift, telling her without reservation that I loved her right back, an outcome Thomas Walther never imagined might arise from bringing a former Nazi to trial.

The Big Story in My Small Life

Testimony Delivered at the Trial of
Oskar Gröning, April 29, 2015

I AM THE CANADIAN CHILD of Holocaust survivors. I'll be speaking to you about the effect on my life of the death of my half-sister, Éva Edit Weinberger, aged six, in Auschwitz in June of 1944. The emotional and psychological difficulties faced by the second generation have been documented in many of the countries that took in most of Europe's post-war Jews. But in Germany, the phenomenon of inherited trauma, or trauma-transfer, is little known because few German Jews survived, and even fewer stayed. Before the Second World War, there had been approximately 550,000 Jews in Germany. By the end of the war, perhaps 15,000 remained. Of these 15,000, most joined the post-war diaspora of displaced European Jews who found new homes around the world. A child of one of these displaced families, I have been asked to talk to you about how the loss of my parents' loved ones, in particular the six-year-old Éva Edit I never knew, left me with a burden of inherited survivor guilt that has been a defining feature of my life. It informed my choice of life partner and the trajectory of my professional endeavours. How these losses shaped me has taken a lifetime to understand.

In June of 1944, almost ten years before my birth, an event took place that could not have been further removed from the world to which

I was to belong. Yet, this event touched me from even the point of conception. The event to which I allude was such an outrage to our sense of ourselves as creatures of compassion and social interdependency, I imagine it capable of fast-tracking its mark to the very genes that came to me from both father and mother. This imprint was in my name, forming my first vague notions of identity. I had been called after two dead children—Éva for my father's daughter of a previous marriage, and Judit after my mother's niece. I am no more aware of the first time I learned this fact than the first time I responded to those sounds. I have always known I am Éva Judit, and also why.

Both these children—Éva Edit Weinberger, aged six, and Judit Borenstein, aged twelve—met their ends in Auschwitz, not the same day, but in the period of fifty-seven days during which 438,000 Hungarian Jews were deported to the camp. The two girls were among the 300,000 gassed, as were Éva's mother, Mancika Mandula Weinberger, aged thirty-four; and my paternal grandparents, Kálmán Weinberger and Ilona Weinberger; their son Pál and his wife, Meri, and their daughter, Marika, aged six; as well as twenty-two other family members in that single transport. All told, my father lost close to eighty relatives. My mother lost her parents, Samuel and Ilona Szwarcz, her sisters Rozsa Szwarcz Borenstein and Magda Szwarcz, her niece Judit Borenstein, and her nephew Tibor Weisz, among numerous aunts, uncles, cousins, and in-laws.

My sister Elaine and I, both born after the war, inherited not jewellery or furniture, but a legacy of two murdered families, ever present in the narratives of our parents and in the photographs and letters penned in the hands of the dead. My father was able to salvage these letters and photos from the mud in the street in front of his home in the town of Nyiregyháza. The house had been taken over, and his personal belongings thrown out into the street. He had escaped from forced labour service with the Hungarian army in November of 1944 and returned home. Mud-splattered letters and photographs were all that was left of mother, father, brothers, wife, and child. He picked up as many as he could stuff into his pockets, and these artifacts became the family my sister Elaine and I grew up with in absentia.

The child, Éva Edit Weinberger, is the one person among my legacy of dead about whom I've been asked to testify today. My life took its shape from her death in ways I have grown to better understand over the last decade and a half, but it needs to be emphasized that she was also just one of the crowd of family members who hung in the wings of my family life in Canada, a gallery of characters against whom my every experience was referenced and compared, who watched us with interest, tenderness, and sometimes dismay. They were alive to us beyond the realm of the imagination, in a way that was almost palpable. When my eldest son was born in 1983, he so much resembled my then seventy-seven-year-old father that my first thought on taking him into my arms was how happy my grandmother would be to see him! Of course, my grandmother, born in 1881, would most likely have been dead by 1983 whether or not she had been murdered by the Nazis. Still, by reflex, I offered my son up to her doting gaze before I phoned my own mother and father.

* * *

In 1979, a book was published by the American author Helen Epstein, which caused a stir among the North American Jewish public. It opened the discussion about the effects on the offspring of Holocaust survivors of their parents' Holocaust history. Helen Epstein had a trove of subjects to study and interview, as about 92,000 post–Second World War Jewish immigrants settled in the United States and about 25,000 in Canada. The cohort of their descendants could be estimated at 250,000. A silence that had shrouded the subject of the Holocaust in many of these families for more than a quarter of a century had been broken. So these were the emotions borne in silence by survivors of the Holocaust—guilt, shame, dread, and mistrust—a silence that had filled their children with unease. Epstein documented the most common experience among survivor families, silence. For reasons of trauma that bred fear, shame, and guilt, the parents who had experienced the horror of the death camps, labour service, cumulative losses of loved ones and homelands, followed for many by the uncertainty of life in displaced persons' camps, silence erected a protective wall. But a wall also imprisons, cutting a person off from emotional connections, locking them in with self-recriminations and fears. Some of these might have been sensed but not fully understood by young children in a household, engendering a kind of inherited anxiety about who their parents were and what once had befallen them. The success of the book *Children of the Holocaust* reflected the deep thirst in the second generation for information about the past and the trauma that had afflicted their parents and their families.

At the time of its publication, my sister Elaine and I read *Children of the Holocaust* with great interest. Our experience as children of Holocaust survivors belonged within the opposite category, perhaps not as numerous as the group locked in silence, but notable in its own right. Instead of silence, these survivors were steeped in the past, speaking of it frequently, and, as in the case of our own parents, sometimes incessantly. In our household, the past and the family members who had populated it felt ever present.

* * *

I'd like to tell you a little about our parents and the circumstances that brought our family to Canada, to give you a better understanding of our family culture of remembrance and veneration of the dead. My father Gusztáv Weinberger Kálmán's family came from the village of Vaja in Szabolcs County in northeastern Hungary. Vaja was named for the Counts of Vay who held their seat in the village and leased approximately three hundred and fifty acres of land, first to my father's grandfather Jakab Szwarcz and then to my grandfather Kálmán Weinberger. It was a large agricultural operation based primarily on the production of tobacco and the distilling of grain alcohol for export. My father and his two younger brothers, Ferenc and Pál, were raised to take over this family business. The extensive group of their relatives belonged to a small Jewish middle

class. The vast majority of Hungarian rural Jews were poor and unedu-
cated, and an extremely wealthy class of Jews held sway in the cities. But
in the countryside of Szabolcs County, the Szwarczes and Weinbergers
were looked to as natural leaders of their community by their wealth,
piety, and, by my father's generation, education. When my father was
called up for forced labour service for the first time in December 1940,
he was almost thirty-five years old, in charge of the finances and many
of the administrative duties of the business, and living in the nearby
town of Nyiregyháza where he had moved with his young family. He
had married Mancika Mandula in 1937. Their daughter, Éva Edit, was
born on April 19, 1938.

My father escaped the sweep of Eichmann's net when the Jews of
northeastern Hungary were among the first to be deported to Auschwitz
after the Germans occupied Hungary at the end of May 1944. He was
away in forced labour, as was his brother Ferenc. Pál, the youngest
brother, at home on leave and recuperating from a hernia operation,
was deported with the others. Ferenc, having survived the death march
out of ghastly conditions in the copper mines in Bor, Serbia, died in the
Flossenburg concentration camp on November 9, 1944, one day before
my father was to arrive home to the family estate near Vaja. My father's
war had ended dramatically. During his last labour service, the men in
his company had, as usual, looked to him for leadership and guidance
during days of chaos. The company was attached to what little was left
of the Hungarian army, which in turn was attached to the retreating
German forces, blowing up bridges over rivers as they crossed westward
in flight from the approaching Russians. Just thirty kilometres from
home, my father had a dread of crossing the Tisza River. To his mind,
once the river was crossed, they would be marched to the train hub town
of Csap, and from there deported to Germany. But the flow of retreating humanity was so heavy that his company was forced over a bridge
earlier than he had expected. The troops mixed chaotically in the town of
Vásárosnameny. The advent of the Russians caused the usual structures
to crumble, and Germans, Hungarians, and Jews broke rank.

My father sought out the Hungarian sergeant in charge of his division. He told him they had to cross back over the bridge, or they'd all end up in Germany. Perhaps the sergeant thought that allegiance to the Germans at this time might not be strategic. What should he say if they were intercepted? Why, answered my father, that the filthy Jews were clogging up the works. Let them go the long way around on the other side. Two hundred Jewish labour servicemen followed my father back over the explosives-lined bridge. No one stopped them or blew them up. My father had liberated himself. Within days, on November 10, 1944, he arrived at the family estate where he found locals had taken up residence. The explanation they gave him was that it made sense to move in once, to quote, "It had pleased the Weinberger family to take off."

My mother, Anna Szwarcz Kalman, became my father's second wife in June 1946. They had met during the previous year after my mother returned to her hometown of Beregszász and found no one left. She had survived Auschwitz, slave labour in munitions factories in Germany, and the long, forced march that led them through Buchenwald, which they again miraculously survived, and eventually towards Dresden. All this time, the starving slaves were herded and driven pointlessly before the retreating SS. Eventually liberated by the Americans, she and her last surviving sister made the torturous journey, sometimes by train, sometimes by truck, but mostly on foot, all the way back to Hungary. Since no other family member had returned to Beregszász, and the Russians were about to seal the re-formed borders enclosing the once-Czech, once-Hungarian town within Ukraine, my mother left. She took with her nothing but the portrait of her favourite sister, Magda, killed by Allied bombs at the munitions plant where the Jewish slaves had been turned out of the barracks so their guards could shelter within.

Having nowhere else to go, she set out for Nyiregyháza, home to her husband Márton Weinberger (name coincidentally the same as my father's). She too had been married before the war, but only a brief few weeks. Márton had been called to labour service and sent to the Russian front. (He was not to reappear until after my sister Elaine was born.)

In Nyiregyháza, presuming Márton dead while in fact he languished in a Russian prisoner of war camp, she met and drew close to my father. By then, he was heading up the local chapter of an organization aiding in the resettlement of Jewish survivors and the location of their missing loved ones. Anna went searching for Márton; instead, she found our father.

A book could be written about the surprising strokes of twisted luck that allowed my parents to outlive their families, and if I digress into their stories, it is because one life's history depends on the lives before it. How to know—or at least imagine—as you and I are asked to do today, Éva Edit Weinberger dead by gas at age six, without at least a snapshot of the family she was born into? And how to explain the effect of her passing on my life lived on a continent six thousand kilometres from her home, without telling you about our shared father, her *Apuka,* who led two hundred men to safety, and my Daddy, a man divided by the great cataclysm that cut his life and his very being in two, leaving him with one foot in the realm of shades and the other on the never quite certain surface of the new world?

In 1956, at the time of the Hungarian Uprising, my father was fifty years old, with a wife thirteen years his junior and two young children, my sister Elaine, age eight, and me, Éva Judit, age two. He was already the patriarch of the remnants of his ravaged family, supporting two mentally unstable elderly aunts and representing for his other surviving relatives the status the Weinbergers had held in Szabolcs County. We lived in Budapest. He had changed his surname, which was too Jewish and German to fit in with the Soviet-aligned interests of post-war Hungary, and now went by his late father's given name Kálmán, which was typically Magyar. He held a position with the Ministry of Agriculture, supervising state-run farms in the countryside outside Budapest. Had it not been for the 1956 revolution, or, more specifically, the reaction the revolution evoked in my mother, my father would never have left Hungary. In fact, if my mother's three surviving siblings had not already emigrated—a brother to Israel, another to London,

England, and her surviving sister to Montreal, Canada—I don't think the subject of emigration would have arisen. Only the force of the argument raised by the revolution could have persuaded my father to leave the homeland in which he was rooted. My mother said she'd had enough of violence. She wanted to raise her children free of oppression and fear. In 1957, having procured exit papers from her siblings in England and Canada, she literally took one child by one hand and the second child by the other and walked us down the path of our apartment house to the sidewalk on Rona *Útca*. Looking over her shoulder to the building against which my father leaned like a limb broken off a massive oak, she announced, "With or without you we are going." He had lost a wife and a child twelve years earlier. At fifty-one years of age, my father started life anew without language, occupation, friends, or familiar points of reference. We spent eighteen months in London, and then moved to Montreal where he lived and eventually died in 1990, leaving a wife, two daughters, and four grandchildren. My mother, Anna, still with us at ninety-five years, continues to follow with interest the development of four great-grandkids. All of us, my sister Elaine and I, our four children, and Elaine's four grandchildren, were born out of the ashes of the sacrificed Éva Edit.

* * *

She looked different from us. Her cousin, Marika, was considered the prettier of the two with her wide round face similar to her father Pál's and our grandmother's, in keeping with the soft curves of the Hungarian ideal. I look more like the little cousin and couldn't see myself as appealing until we returned to visit Hungary in 1969 where I was made much of. At home in Montreal, we aspired to look hungry, big-eyed, and boyish like the British model of the times, Twiggy. However I may have starved myself, my face stayed full and my cheekbones non-existent. Évike, as she was known by the family, would have more likely grown into the Western proportions of beauty. Her face was a small oval. In one photo she strikes me as a total stranger, looking like no one but herself, delicate in build, and with large eyes alight with quickness. Her hair is in two braids looped loosely and tied up in white ribbons on either side of a centre part. A downy growth of new hair spills from beneath the upswept braids onto her generous forehead. In one photo with her mother, they both smile flirtatiously at the photographer. Was it our father? In another favourite of mine, I see in her image someone dear and totally unrelated, a psychotherapist who helped me through one of the darkest periods of my life. I realize I've had a lifetime habit of seeing Évike in women I look up to. She would have been the same age as a teacher-mentor I met in college, a woman of Central European and half-Jewish extraction. When she was my instructor, I often wondered if Évike would have grown up into a brilliant teacher like her. Like my mentor, Évike had taught herself to read and write by the age of four. Her letters to my father during his labour service are charmingly printed, the words running together without spaces in between but almost all correctly spelled. She would have been so much brighter and more talented than I was, I concluded. In graduate school, I studied with a prominent author. She, too, was influential in my development and, again, born the same year as Évike. I saw in these women a potential that might have been hers had my half-sister been afforded the opportunity that was her right, to grow into adulthood. Although I soon overtook Évike in age, I didn't see her as increasingly younger, but rather sixteen years my senior, ever projected into the future to which she was entitled. The third picture on my desk is not one I would have selected. Herr Walther, our legal representative to this court, had it enlarged for me and my sister Elaine. In it, Évike looks deeply anxious. Her brows are puckered, and she clings to the teddy bear she holds in every photograph. Perhaps the sun is too bright, but it is hard not to imagine that she is gazing at the future. In all these photos, I look for a point of resemblance that connects us. But except for the high forehead and finely etched mouth, I see none.

How much then did Évike and I share? In what way, if any, may I have embodied a part of her?

* * *

As a child, I formed a strange myth to explain the baffling circumstances of my existence. There must have been something wrong about the old, beautiful way of life that my father extolled in his idealized narratives of the past. According to Gusztáv, his parents could not have been more devoted to each other, their children, and their numerous relations. His mother, Ilona, was a paragon of religious faith and observance; his father, Kálmán, unstintingly honest in affairs of business, wise, fair-minded, and forward-thinking; his brothers intelligent and accomplished, Pál especially in having earned a doctorate in law. The Szwarczes on his mother's side had been renowned over four generations for their philanthropy and hospitality, each exemplary in his or her own way, but perhaps most so his grandfather, Jakab, a proponent of innovation and an early adopter of new technologies. The clan had been sophisticated and good. Good. Yet, if so, asked the child-skeptic born to him for life in a different world, why were they all wiped out? A child raised to believe in a beneficent God, but above all, because of her father's carefully wrought narratives, in a causality that gave shape and meaning to life. Surely, surely something must not have been right with that world for it to have been so summarily, brutally, and irrevocably eclipsed.

I came up with an answer that makes sense only to a child. For some reason, my sister Elaine and I had to be born. If we were meant to be, then it followed that Évike and her world were not. It was that simple. I could imagine no circumstance that would have allowed all three of us life. My father, a committed family man with a deeply conservative nature, would never have divorced Mancika to marry Anna, a younger woman. Nor would he have ever wished to, even had his path crossed with Anna's in an alternate universe. Gusztáv and Mancika were happily married, much better suited to each other in temperament by his accounts, than what we witnessed of his relationship with our mother. No. In order for Gusztáv and Anna to find each other, Mancika and Évike, and in fact their whole society, steeped in tradition and precedence, had to go. That Évike might have miraculously survived in Auschwitz without her mother, to be reclaimed by our father after the war, and brought up under one roof with me and Elaine (far-fetched a notion as this might be), had never occurred to me until it was recently brought to my attention by an objective outsider, John, spouse of my later life, whose vision on this subject isn't emotionally clouded. Even at my current age, I resist the logic.

Early on, through my father's stories and my mother's startling revelations of horror, I absorbed the knowledge that innocent children could be murdered and whole families and communities eradicated by forces beyond their control. I might be playing with a doll that said, "Mama." When I took the doll's clothes off, the mechanical voice box lodged in her back was exposed. My mother, happening to pass by, would exclaim, "Don't show me that. It reminds me of my cousin Márta when we were running under the bombs like ants, and I ran by her, her back blown open from shrapnel." Such unexpected statements were not uncommon for my mother. If she was in the mood to reminisce, I say this sarcastically I'm afraid, she might go from that memory to another that involved a synopsis of how other members of Márta's family had met their ends. We didn't know when my mother's memories might detonate or what might trigger them. It felt like setting off a landmine buried in the most peaceful of fields. The world plainly could be a scary place. As a young emigrant of three and a half, I, too, was swept up in the migration of peoples. What could I carry with me as an emblem of the safety and faith I needed so as to flourish and grow? I suspect it was around this time that my personal creation myth emerged. I decided that the old, beautiful world had been a false start. As in a race when one runner darts ahead of the signal and all runners must return to the line to begin again, so, too, with that world and mine. It had all been a false start, including Évike, the innocent precursor of fate, who had leapt ahead of the whistle. She was the child who was not meant to be because those who were, Elaine and I, had not yet arrived at the starting line. From this hypothesis, the solution to the terrors that might befall us followed. Everything bad that could happen to a family had already struck my father and mother. The dangerous times had come before and thus wouldn't come again. Elaine and I, by extension, had been inoculated against disaster. The suffering that as humans we continue to inflict on one another defy our understanding as adults, let alone that of a child. I offer that in my defense, as well as the ego-centric world view native to early childhood. But why did these personal myths retain their hold? Why did I not grow out of them, or even become aware of their influence until middle age?

* * *

To answer these questions—not that I am so important that you need to know much about my psychology—but if you are to see how the effects of trauma on one generation made themselves felt on the next, I must tell you a little more about my father.

Before the war, Gusztáv Weinberger was a leader within his rural Jewish community. He held a degree in agronomy from the Royal Hungarian Agricultural Academy in Debrecen. He then apprenticed for two years on the estate owned by his mother's cousins, the Rochlitzes, in Nagyvársány, not more than twenty kilometres from his home. The Rochlitzes were distinctive on two counts. They had been landowners from a time when it was rare for Jews to be permitted to own land, and they were freethinking, neither religious nor traditionally observant. They came from a line of intellectuals and early feminists. Living with the Rochlitzes, the twenty-year-old Gusztáv's world view broadened, laying a foundation for his eventual life in Canada. With the Rochlitzes, Gusztáv ate *tréf*, non-kosher foods, including pork. He grew to admire women who cut their hair short as an expression of emancipation. And as part of his training, he learned to keep the complex accounts of a business enterprise larger than that of his family in Vaja. The close relationship Gusztáv developed with the Rochlitzes resumed in Canada after he reconnected with the only surviving member of that family. Zsuzsa Rochlitz is now a ninety-year-old grandmother. She was the only one to survive from the transport from the Kisvarda Ghetto that delivered my father's thirty-four relatives and loved ones to Auschwitz, the only one besides my father who could provide first-hand testimony about Évike and her mother Mancika. I wish Zsuzsa Rochlitz were here today to report to you about her remarkable family, her beloved parents Zoltán and Jancsika, and her younger brother Péter. They all perished, her father shot; her mother, having passed herself off as Zsuzsa's sister and strong enough to work, died in Auschwitz later, after Zsuzsa was separated from her and sent to a munitions plant. Péter died on a death march alongside my uncle Pál, also some months on. Zsuzsa, Jancsika, Pál, and Péter were the only ones of the thirty-four family members in that single transport to survive Mengele's initial selection; Zsuzsa was the only one to come through the war.

I cannot emphasize enough the ties that bound my father and Zsuzsa by dint of being the last ones left standing. Over the years, a handful of the large clan resurfaced—in Sydney, Boston, and New York. He treated them like royalty, but no one more so than Zsuzsa who represented not so much the little girl he had given sweets to on the Rochlitz estate, but her mother and especially her father whom he had loved and revered. In Canada, deprived of familiar bearings, most of all his identity within that diminished community, my father clung to these remaining relations much in the way he clung to the dead.

Before my birth, my father filled my sister Elaine's head and heart with frequent narratives about his dead loved ones. Elaine was born in 1947. Still an only child, she could identify his photographs, reciting like a catechism the names of the dead. I cannot imagine how he was able to start a second family so soon upon losing everyone. Life pushes us on. Swept along in a tide, we grab at anything to keep afloat. I think that the guilt of survival my father carried in him, threatening always to drag him under, could be measured by the flow of narration and remembrance that poured out of him almost uninterruptedly over the years. The stories flowed with a fluency of structure that suggested he was always composing them somewhere in his being. I would not go so far as to say he took a conscious stab at making art. I imagine the stories somehow internally wrote themselves. He did not watch television. He read the local newspapers and Hungarian novels and the occasional novel in English if it was about a subject related to Jewry, the war, or the Hungarian experience. My father would have been shocked to be called a writer manqué or even a raconteur. He simply shared his recollections, memories that played on the screen of his mind like a living movie he then played back to us in words.

The father of my childhood did not work as an agronomist. After two years in Canada, my mother took an intensive college course to re-certify herself as a schoolteacher so that she might work for the public school system. My father could not bring himself to do the same in his field. He might work for a government ministry, my mother urged, as he had in Budapest. Just a few courses would do it. He was too old, my father said. Too old to learn the technical language, too old to have the energy, too old to successfully transplant in new soil. The father I remember always claimed to be old, and it's true, compared to the young, short-sleeved, cigarette-smelling fathers of my Canadian friends, he did look old. Old and foreign. My father wore cardigans or suit jackets and did not go out in public in shirt sleeves. He always wore a fedora to work and carried a briefcase for his lunch and newspaper. He had a stoop to his back from spinal tuberculosis in childhood. He was often mistaken for my grandfather. He was not the same father little Évike had flirted with in her photograph. He worried about snowstorms and daughters walking home from the bus stop after dark.

We lived in a new suburb in the east end of Montreal, far from the neighbourhoods where Jews had settled. I was the only Jew in my elementary school and the only Jew in high school. We ate tréf as he had learned to enjoy at the Rochlitzes as a young man. My mother wore her thick hair short for his pleasure. He worked as a bookkeeper for a Jewish firm in the clothing industry downtown. He often remarked that one could never know how useful incidental skills might turn out to be. He had learned to keep the books for the Rochlitzes, never imagining that he would end up making his living that way for a quarter of a century. When we rode the buses together on Saturday mornings, he to put in his half day at work, and I to go to a Jewish school in the west end where my parents hoped I'd acquire a taste for Jewish company, I felt an urge to protect him from the judgment of the French and English Canadians riding with us who heard him speaking Hungarian. They might look down on him as some-one foreign and 'other.' They had no idea who he was, who he had been, a man of stature, of the world, or, of another world. It seemed poignantly ironic that he missed the place where he could be his natural self, that place that had cast his family as 'other' in the extreme, an 'other' that was hardly human, so 'other' they didn't deserve life; yet here in a freer society where he could own property, educate his children, and qualify to work in any field he chose, he felt so utterly out of step with his milieu he never stopped seeing himself as out of place and set apart.

* * *

Now, finally, I will speak about second-generation survivor guilt. Évike's death shaped my life so fundamentally, I wasn't to understand or even recognize it until I was well into middle age and had experienced trag-edy first-hand. Her death was part of me as were the genes I'd inherited, and I was as unaware of its influence as we are unaware of what resides in most of our genomes. What I was conscious of was that I had had a sister whom I'd supplanted, and who might have turned out to be more successful in a professional sense than I did; on the other hand, a sister who had to be replaced because fate somehow had pre-ordained me. I felt I must amount to great things in order to justify the forfeiture of her life, even as I understood myself to be cramped by limitations.

All my life I planned to be a writer. In second grade I was president of the class's little literature club. At the age of ten, I announced I was going to grow up to be an English teacher who wrote books. My modest gift was recognized by various teachers through the years, notably, my mentor in college. In that class, I met my future husband, a young man with a prodigious work ethic and a flare for writing. We were very young when we moved in together. We had two children, and lived together for twenty-five years.

As far back as I can remember realizing that I think most clearly with a pen in my hand, I intended to write the story of my father's family. This at last would solve the riddle of my existence, why I was meant to be. Through my words, his dead loved ones would once again come to life. In fact, I've been able to write only the story of myself.

In May 2000, two months ahead of his forty-fourth birthday, my husband of twenty-five years took his life. He had battled depression as long as I had known him, but in the last five years, the illness became unmanageable. At this time, I sought the support of a psychotherapist in learning to manage life with a very sick partner and two children. Following my husband's suicide, I tried to understand my marriage, what had led me into it, and what had kept me from leaving. These explorations brought me back to my half-sister Évike. I came to understand that my choice of a life partner had been predicated on guilt. A child had died so that I might supplant her. How better to expiate such a debt than by saving someone who might otherwise not survive without me? My husband was hardly more than a seventeen-year-old boy when we met. Not long after, he suddenly left his home and his family, refusing all contact with them. He was young, raw, alone in the world, hyper-sensitive, and vulnerable. He stood by his convictions and his friends, worked harder than anyone else in our class, and wrote like a dream. This was one worthy soul, I saw at a glance, who deserved only the best life could offer, but instead he had been dealt a bad hand, as he used to say, in the form of a condition that made him doubt himself at every turn. I recognized him right away, one of the exceptional people, like the members of my father's family, who had been dealt a hand that was terminal.

Of course, I couldn't have known that my husband's hand would prove terminal as well. What I understood was that it was my fate to save him. Essentially, for twenty-five years, I provided around-the-clock care.

Helping my husband make a life amounted to helping him stay alive. This was a role I never questioned, however it hemmed me in, consumed my mental and physical energies, and drew on my creative strengths. I was indebted, after all. I owed my life literally to the deaths of all the fine souls who had been unjustifiably murdered. The least I could do was save this one who also deserved his chance.

I was twenty-six when my sister Elaine, trained as a historian, came to me with a proposition. She planned to tape-record our father telling the story of his life. She would do the historical research if I turned our father's narratives into a book. She was giving me the opportunity to write the book I had always intended. For a couple of years, we collaborated on translating my father's recordings into English, spending many hours on the telephone, me in western Canada at the time and she in Montreal, discussing the personalities of the characters in my father's dramatis personae, and the shape the book might take. My late husband said something then that stopped me in my tracks, totally out of keeping with his considerate nature. He said, "Why do you think anyone would be interested in the story of your family? After all, it's not as if they accomplished anything special or that anyone's ever heard of them."

He was saying what I had always felt riding the buses with my father under the suspicious eyes of our Canadian neighbours. We were little people of no great count. The world had tried to get rid of us. Who would care about my father's stories from another continent and era that held little relevance to Canadians? I persuaded Elaine to write the book herself, which, wisely, she did. It was easier than attempting my grand design and failing, as I was bound to, to raise the dead. A myth created too early in life to know what I was doing demanded frequent reinforcement: Évike had died for my right to live; in turn, my other rights were of small consequence.

I would never have written the book Elaine imagined and then wrote. Eventually, as my husband's illness progressed, I saw the imperative of making something for myself. I wrote a collection of stories that drew on the narratives we had translated together. But this book turned out to be about me, Éva Judit, the child of Holocaust survivors, not about its actual victims.

It doesn't sit with me comfortably to address this court in the form of a victim impact statement. The effects of the Holocaust on my life can't be put on a par with how it changed my parents and all those who suffered its ravages. If I am at all a victim, it is in a titular sense. The loss to me of Éva Edit Weinberger pales by comparison with the devastation her death wrought on our father. Most of my dramas, my difficulties integrating and assimilating into a new culture through a second language, for instance, were measured against the superhuman challenges my parents had faced. When things went wrong for me, I tended to undermine them as trivial. Theirs loomed so large, their world, my father's pre-war world in particular, felt more real. In some ways, I had difficulty fully inhabiting my life, recognizing the richness of my sensations, perceptions, and experiences. Instead, these came to me as dim reflections of my father's Platonic ideal. Yet, I grew up into a strong individual who has never felt anything but gratitude for the stroke of tragic chance that had given me breath. Mine is not the voice of a victim. We were a family of loud voices—the deep, narrating voice of my father, my mother's shrill voice trying to draw our attention away from him, and my sister's and mine, clamouring to be known.

Whenever I took up my pen, my insistent voice leapt to the fore, tattooing me to the page. It came from a place of self-preservation, affirming the here and now. The last thing I would ever have imagined would be to use this voice to address a German court about the phantom child whose shadow preceded me through the years. I cannot fully express how liberating it feels to have her acknowledged so publicly and to be heard on behalf of my father and mother, little people who bore the enormous weight of history without the solace of recognition.

My psychotherapist left me an invaluable gift that helped me go forward after my husband took his life. I could no more have saved him than my father or any of the survivors of the Holocaust could have saved their dear ones. It's easy to say they should all have left at the first signs of Nazi sabre-rattling. Hindsight showed me too, some steps I might have taken that might have forestalled the outcome of my husband's illness. But such thoughts are akin to blaming the victims. In the moment, in the ever-flowing now, we're too close to our situations to see them clearly or in their entirety. We use our best judgment given the information available within the parameters of the present. My therapist was a believer in a principle of learning how to look at traumatic experience in a new way, one that allows us to co-exist with the trauma, if not more comfortably, then at least without it getting in the way of our daily life. After my husband died, I suffered panic attacks that kept me from sleeping. In particular, I had difficulty with images of his death. My therapist and I debated the principle of looking at trauma from a different perspective in order to see it in a new light. I insisted this was a type of lie, like the re-writing of history for propaganda purposes. What happened *happened* and could not be changed. How, for instance I demanded, could I ever contemplate the image of my half-sister Évike and her mother in the gas chamber without succumbing to despair?

My father's cousin, Zsuzsa Rochlitz, was almost twenty years old when she was stuffed into the cattle car bound for Auschwitz. Like everyone else in it, family, friends, and strangers, she was overwhelmed by the appalling stench and accompanying terror that for most of them would be their next-to-last experience on earth. Although she was comforted by her mother Jancsika, Zsuzsa's stunned attention fixed upon another mother-daughter pair. She tells us that throughout that hideous journey, she never once saw Mancika Mandula Weinberger falter in her reassurance of her six-year-old daughter Évike. Over and over, she consoled her calmly. Perhaps where they were going, they would meet up with Évike's *Apuka*. Her father would be waiting. They would all three be together again. Zsuzsa might have been so impressed with Gusztáv's wife's reassuring composure and resolve that she took comfort in it herself. She, too, tried to believe that her dear cousin Gusztáv, who always had time for her when she was a little girl and he an apprentice on her father's estate, would join them. Perhaps the image of Gusztáv was a talisman of hope and magical thinking under desperate conditions. Somehow, like Évike, she had to believe that once Gusztáv was with them, they would be all right. Zsuzsa, in her Canadian life, worked in infant care at a government agency for new immigrants. She always told us, "I never met a woman who better epitomized sensitive, intelligent, and respectful mothering than your father's wife Mancika as she calmed her darling child during that dreadful journey."

I look again at Herr Walther's photograph of Évike. She is trying to smile, even as her eyes and brows pull together anxiously. Her lovely high forehead is deeply furrowed. It's hard for me to look into her face. Each gossamer hair in the fringe spilling out of her gathered braids attests to the teeming abundance of life within her. The wispy promise of each strand is as difficult to contemplate as the image of this little girl naked, enfolded by the naked flesh that gave birth to her, as together they slide to the floor of the devil's own bathhouse. I glowered angrily at my therapist. What a lie and betrayal to consider re-formulating this excruciating image into something palatable to live with!

"But," she said reaching for my two hands. She had taken the hands of my sixteen-year-old son in this same way when she had offered him her condolences upon the death of his father. "You are like that woman, don't you know? Despite the toll on you of your husband's descent into madness, your dedication to your children didn't waver."

Since her words, I've learned to co-exist with this image of horror, along with other memories absorbed as through a membrane from father and mother. I couldn't save my husband. Nor have I located any resemblance in me to my precocious, delicate, half-sister Éva Edit Weinberger, irrevocably lost. But one intrinsic quality belonging to one of the sacrificed innocents, a woman not even related to me by blood, had clung improbably—fine and fierce as spider's silk—to the host it had found.

Acknowledgements

THIS BOOK WOULD NOT have been written had Thomas Walther not brought the former SS officer, Oskar Gröning, to trial. I'd probably still be hitting dead-ends, trying to figure out what I need to write. To Jo-Ann Wallace, friend, writer, reader of first drafts, thanks for coming along on this ride; it wouldn't be the same the book without you. My sister Elaine Kalman-Naves, collaborator of a lifetime of navigating our parents' past, thanks for clearing the path. Barbara Pulling, whose work through the various drafts, and imprint on the structure of this memoir were invaluable, thanks also for support during the fallow years.

Ken Whyte and the team at Sutherland House made the publishing process feel like a breeze, never letting me feel like a supplicant, nor asking me to jump through hoops I wasn't trained for: deep-felt thanks. Julia McIntosh at Library Archives Canada went above and beyond the call of duty in her assistance with research regarding Miss Catherine Jackson of Rawdon, Quebec.

The hardest years were utterly redeemed by my sons, each of whom was a joy to raise, regardless of circumstances. Whenever the clouds lifted, it was their doing. Their late father and I could never have thanked them enough. Lieba Lesk ferried me safely back over the River Styx to the land of the living. If only she were still here to thank again. Running on empty, my late husband was nonetheless able to give so much. I'll be forever in his debt for the life we built together. My parents, Anna Schwartz Kalman, and the late Gusztav Weinberger Kalman: my story and my love rests on theirs.

It was John Trainor's idea that I consider going to Germany to testify at the trial of Oskar Gröning. I have him to thank for showing me the door that had opened, and for accompanying me every step of the way. Without him, and everything he has brought into my life, this book would not have been written.

Journal Acknowledgements

Several chapters appeared under different titles and in altered forms in the following publications: "Coming to the Table" and "Spilling the Beans" as "Testifying" in *Another Chicago Magazine*; "In Sickness and in Health," in *STORGY Magazine*; "Red" in *Barzakh Magazine*; "Hindsight Comes too Late" as "About Time" in *The Nasiona*; "Post-Cards from the Land of the Oppressors" as "Us and Them" in *Die Letzten NS-Verfahren* (The Last National Socialist Procedures); an abridged version of the Oskar Gröning Nazi War Crimes Trial testimony in BBC online; "*La Campagne*" in *Bluestem*; "Strange Bedfellows" in *Iris Literary Journal*.